Colonial Williamsburg

THE GUIDE

THE OFFICIAL COMPANION TO THE HISTORIC AREA

Colonial Williamsburg

THE COLONIAL WILLIAMSBURG FOUNDATION
WILLIAMSBURG, VIRGINIA

Globe Pequot

GUILFORD, CONNECTICUT

2030 29 28 27 26 25 24 23 22 21 20 19   1 2 3 4 5 6

Library of Congress Cataloging-in-Publication Data

Names: Colonial Williamsburg Foundation.
Title: Colonial Williamsburg : the Guide ; the Official Companion to the Historic Area
    published by the Colonial Williamsburg Foundation, Williamsburg, Virginia,
    and Globe Pequot, Guilford, Connecticut / the Colonial Williamsburg Foundation.
Description: Williamsburg, Virginia : Colonial Williamsburg Foundation, 2019.
    | Includes index.
Identifiers: LCCN 2019004813| ISBN 9780879352974 (pbk. : alk. paper) | ISBN 9781493048229
Subjects: LCSH: Colonial Williamsburg (Williamsburg, Va.)—Guidebooks. | Williamsburg (Va.)—
    Guidebooks. | Historic sites—Interpretive programs—Virginia—Williamsburg.
Classification: LCC F234.W7 C66 2019 | DDC 975.5/4252—dc23 LC record available at
https://lccn.loc.gov/2019004813

Art directed by Katherine Jordan
Designed by Katie Appel
Digital imaging by Tom Green

Published by
The Colonial Williamsburg Foundation
PO Box 1776
Williamsburg, VA 23187
colonialwilliamsburg.org

Globe Pequot
An imprint of Rowman & Littlefield Publishing Group, Inc.
GlobePequot.com
Distributed by NATIONAL BOOK NETWORK

Printed in the United States of America

CONTENTS

Want to know what led Patrick Henry to declare, "If this be treason, make the most of it"?

Ask him.

Or how an enslaved servant might have felt about a declaration of independence that promises "all men are created equal"?

Ask her.

Want to know what kind of hair a perukemaker uses for a wig?

Feel it.

Or what was served at an eighteenth-century coffeehouse?

Taste it.

Or what it's like to fire the same kind of musket used by soldiers during the American Revolution?

Try it.

This is living history, where you experience the sights and sounds and smells and tastes of colonial and Revolutionary America. And the ideas, too—for it was in Williamsburg, the capital of the largest colony in British America, that democracy took root.

In the Historic Area of Colonial Williamsburg, you can see hundreds of restored, reconstructed, and historically furnished buildings. You can meet the men and women—black, white, and Native American, enslaved and free— who built a new nation. And you can discover connections between past and present that reveal the enduring relevance of America's founding documents and principles.

Getting Here

Williamsburg is midway between Richmond and Norfolk on Interstate 64. Take exit 238 and then follow signs to the Colonial Williamsburg Regional Visitor Center.

The nearest airport serving commercial airlines is Newport News–Williamsburg International Airport (PHF), about twenty-five minutes away. Richmond International Airport (RIC) is about forty-five minutes away, and Norfolk International Airport (ORF) is about an hour away. Amtrak and Greyhound serve the Williamsburg Transportation Center, which is just blocks from the Historic Area.

Colonial Williamsburg Regional Visitor Center

The Historic Area is more than three hundred acres, and there is no single right way to visit it. A good place to start is the Visitor Center, where you will find ample free parking. You can buy tickets at several Colonial Williamsburg ticketing locations, but the Visitor Center staff can also help you plan your visit, select the appropriate tickets, and make reservations for dining, lodging, and special programs. At the Visitor Center, you can see *Williamsburg—The Story of a Patriot*, a movie dramatizing events in Williamsburg on the eve of the American Revolution.

As you leave the Visitor Center, you will find buses that run continuously to the Historic Area. You can alternatively walk from the Visitor Center to the Historic Area—a quarter-mile path takes you back in time to the eighteenth century.

The Visitor Center also has information on other area attractions, including Jamestown and Yorktown.

Touring the Historic Area

The Historic Area has hundreds of original and reconstructed houses, shops, public buildings, and outbuildings. Some are open to ticketed guests while others are currently used as private residences and administrative offices. Some you tour in a group; some you tour on your own, but interpreters are available to answer questions. Shops and dining taverns are open to the public.

Sites are generally open 9 a.m. to 5 p.m. with special programming in the evening. Not all sites are open every day, and not all sites are open all day. A flag near a building's entrance indicates that the site is open.

For the latest information on schedules and programs, go to colonialwilliamsburg.org or download the free official app.

To buy tickets or for more information, go to the Visitor Center, the Lumber House Ticket Office, or the Merchants Square Ticket office; visit colonialwilliamsburg.org; or call 1-800-HISTORY. Tickets are also available at the Art Museums of Colonial Williamsburg and, for hotel guests, at the Williamsburg Inn and the Williamsburg Lodge.

Public Buildings

It was in these buildings that America's founders met to discuss independence, to debate the nature of the new nation, to worship—and also to eat, discuss business, and hear the latest news and gossip.

Bruton Parish Church. SEE PAGE 96.
Capitol. SEE PAGE 19.
Courthouse. SEE PAGE 64.
Governor's Palace. SEE PAGE 81.
Magazine. SEE PAGE 64.
Market House. SEE PAGE 62.
Public Gaol. SEE PAGE 49.
Public Hospital. SEE PAGE 101.
Raleigh Tavern. SEE PAGE 31.
R. Charlton's Coffeehouse. SEE PAGE 22.
Wetherburn's Tavern. SEE PAGE 36.

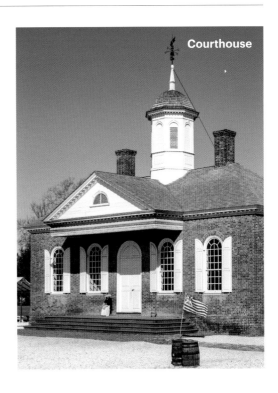

Courthouse

Private Homes

The houses of the Historic Area offer a look at eighteenth-century architecture and furnishings and also at the lives of the gentry, of the "middling sort," and of the free and enslaved black residents of Williamsburg.

George Wythe House. SEE PAGE 86.
Great Hopes Plantation. SEE PAGE 77.
James Geddy House. SEE PAGE 92.
Peyton Randolph House. SEE PAGE 72.
Thomas Everard House. SEE PAGE 90.

Trades

Colonial Williamsburg's tradespeople are among the best traditional artisans in the nation. They use period techniques and tools to make re-creations of period products. Unlike other costumed interpreters, they do not portray eighteenth-century characters or speak in eighteenth-century dialects.

Wheelwright

Apothecary. SEE PAGE 27.
Blacksmith. SEE PAGE 55.
Bookbinder. SEE PAGE 58.
Brickmaker. SEE PAGE 72.
Cabinetmaker. SEE PAGE 70.
Carpenter. SEE PAGE 51.
Cooper. SEE PAGE 89.
Foodways. SEE PAGE 82.
Foundry. SEE PAGE 94.
Gunsmith. SEE PAGE 44.
Historic Farmer. SEE PAGE 70.
Historic Gardener. SEE PAGE 97.
Joiner. SEE PAGE 99.
Leatherworker. SEE PAGE 55.
Milliner and Mantua-maker. SEE PAGE 34.
Printer. SEE PAGE 58.
Shoemaker. SEE PAGE 95.
Silversmith. SEE PAGE 33.
Tailor. SEE PAGE 100.
Tin shop. SEE PAGES 55–56.
Weaver. SEE PAGE 94.
Wheelwright. SEE PAGE 86.
Wigmaker. SEE PAGE 29.

Museums

At the newly expanded Art Museums of Colonial Williamsburg, see thousands of works, including American and British fine, decorative, and mechanical art; American folk art; archaeological artifacts; and architectural fragments. Bassett Hall was home to John D. Rockefeller Jr. and Abby Aldrich Rockefeller.

DeWitt Wallace Decorative Arts Museum.
SEE PAGE 104.
Abby Aldrich Rockefeller Folk Art Museum.
SEE PAGE 110.
Bassett Hall. SEE PAGE 43.

Edith Cumbo

Nation Builders

In Colonial Williamsburg's Historic Area you will encounter many costumed interpreters. Of special interest are those called "Nation Builders." These interpreters portray eighteenth-century figures who made significant contributions to America's enduring story.

Aggie of Turkey Island, an enslaved woman who sued for her freedom and that of her children.

Edith Cumbo, one of a handful of free blacks who lived in Williamsburg during the Revolution.

Patrick Henry, a patriot famed for his stirring oratory.

Thomas Jefferson, a student and then a member of the House of Burgesses in Williamsburg.

James Armistead Lafayette, an enslaved man who spied for the Continental army.

Marquis de Lafayette, a French officer who volunteered for the Continental army and played a key role in the Revolution.

James Madison, who secured passage for Jefferson's Virginia Statute for Religious Freedom before becoming the "father of the Constitution" and the fourth president.

George Mason, who drafted the Virginia Declaration of Rights, which stated that "all men are by nature equally free and independent."

Gowan Pamphlet, an enslaved tavern worker who founded a Baptist church for blacks, portrayed both as a young man and a visionary pastor.

Clementina Rind, who after her husband's death took over the publication of the *Virginia Gazette*.
Ann Wager, a teacher at the Bray School for African American children in Williamsburg.
George Washington, who is portrayed as a colonel of the Virginia Regiment and as commander in chief of the Continental army and later the first president.
Martha Washington, who provided essential support to George as general and as president.
George Wythe, a leading lawyer and scholar, a signer of the Declaration of Independence, and a mentor to Jefferson.

Gardens

Colonial Williamsburg's Historic Area gardens range from the formal splendor of the Governor's Palace gardens to utilitarian kitchen gardens. Even gardens attached to private residences are generally open to the public. Below are some of the most popular gardens.

Alexander Craig House
Alexander Purdie House
Benjamin Powell House
Bracken Tenement
Bryan House

Christiana Campbell's Tavern
Colonial Garden
David Morton House
Elizabeth Carlos House
George Reid House
George Wythe House
Governor's Palace
John Blair House
Orlando Jones House
Palmer House
Prentis House
Taliaferro-Cole House
Wetherburn's Tavern

For Families

The entire Historic Area is family friendly, but some options are especially appealing to kids. Note that some of these are open seasonally; check colonialwilliamsburg.org for the schedules.

Candlelit concert at
the Governor's Palace

Evening Programs

The Historic Area is alive after nightfall with family-friendly entertainment including singing and dancing, theater and storytelling, witches and ghosts. Check colonialwilliamsburg.org to see what is available at the time of your visit.

Highlights for First-Time Guests

Your own interests may lead you to particular sites, but if this is your first visit, consider these:

Art Museums. SEE PAGE 102.
Blacksmith. SEE PAGE 55.
Capitol. SEE PAGE 19.
Courthouse. SEE PAGE 64.
Governor's Palace. SEE PAGE 81.
Magazine. SEE PAGE 64.
Peyton Randolph House. SEE PAGE 72.

Accessibility

Colonial Williamsburg's "Guide for Guests with Disabilities" provides a detailed description of services and facilities available, including parking, restroom locations, wheelchair rentals, telephone assistance, transportation facilities, service animals, sign language interpreters, movie captioning, headsets, and other auxiliary aides. It is available at the Visitor Center.

For more information, contact:

Colonial Williamsburg Regional Visitor Center
101-A Visitor Center Drive
Williamsburg, Virginia 23185
(888) 965-7254

SEE AND DO ▶

▶

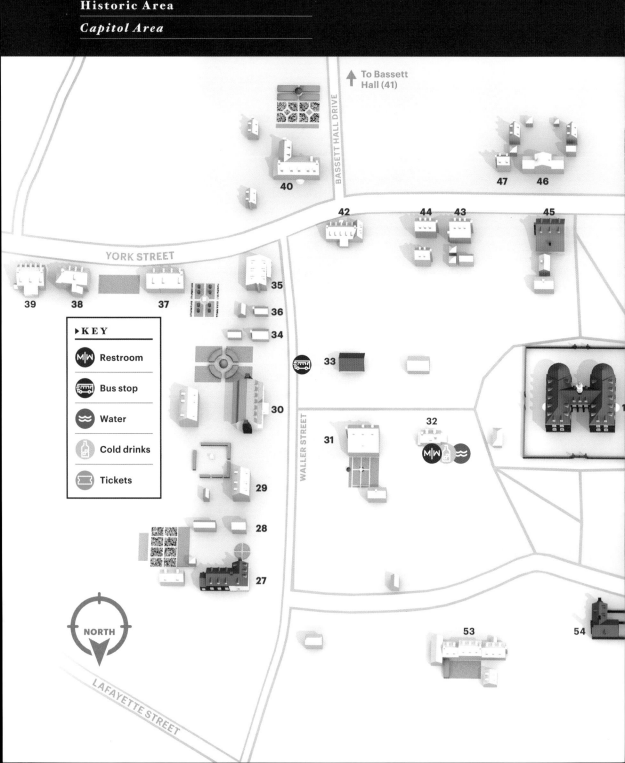

To Bassett
Hall (41)

BASSETT HALL DRIVE

40

47   46

42   44   43   45

YORK STREET

39   38   37   35

36

34

▶ KEY

M|W Restroom

Bus stop

Water

Cold drinks

Tickets

33

30

32

31   M|W

29

28

27

NORTH

53   54

LAFAYETTE STREET

WALLER STREET

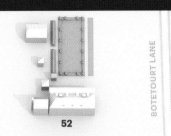

BOTETOURT LANE

52

FRANCIS STREET

48

49

50

51

BLAIR STREET

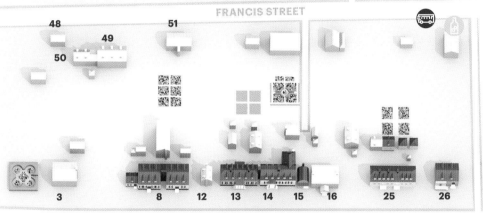

3

8

12

13

14

15

16

25

26

DUKE OF GLOUCESTER STREET

4

5

6

7

9

10

11

17

19

20

21

23

24

18

22

BOTETOURT STREET

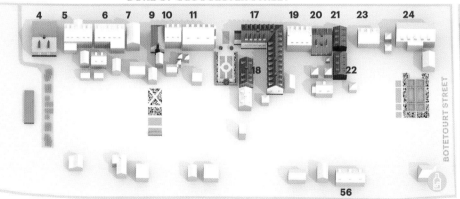

56

NICHOLSON STREET

55

57

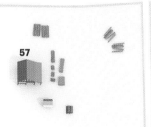

Duke of Gloucester Street

1 Capitol
Open to ticket holders

To many colonists, the Stamp Act of 1765 trampled on a fundamental right: that only their elected assemblies could tax them. In May, the twenty-nine-year-old Patrick Henry addressed the Virginia House of Burgesses at the Capitol. He exclaimed, according to an 1817 biography: "Caesar had his Brutus—Charles the first, his Cromwell—and George the third . . ." At this point, Henry was interrupted by cries of "Treason!" He responded without hesitation: "If this be treason, make the most of it."

Some historians have questioned whether these were Henry's exact words, but almost all agree that his speech stirred the burgesses to pass resolutions condemning the act of Parliament. Henry's words inspired Virginians to defend their liberties and moved the colony toward revolution.

Eleven years later, Virginia's representatives—again meeting in the Capitol, but now as members of the Fifth Virginia Convention instead of as burgesses—instructed their delegates to the Continental Congress to propose independence. In May 1776, while Congress debated Virginia's motion, the Virginia Convention went ahead and severed ties with Great Britain. The Convention then adopted a Declaration of Rights, which acknowledged such principles as power derived from the people, the right to a trial by jury, prohibition of cruel and unusual punishments, and freedom of religion.

In June of that year, the Convention adopted a constitution that established a new government for Virginia with a governor, a bicameral legislature, and a court system. The delegates then elected Henry governor of the commonwealth.

The Capitol has an H-shaped plan with two wings that reflect the division of power in the colonial government between the elected members of the House of Burgesses and the royal governor and his Council, who were all appointed to lifetime tenure by the king. In addition to serving as the administrative head of colonial government, the royal governor and Council exercised control as the upper house of Virginia's legislature and as the justices in the General Court, the highest court in the colony, which met on the first floor of the west wing. When meeting in their executive and legislative roles, these powerful gentlemen made use of the Council Chamber, the most ornate room in the building, on the second floor of the west wing.

The House of Burgesses met in a large yet relatively simple chamber on the first floor in the east wing of the Capitol and also made use of the committee rooms on the second floor. Burgesses were elected to represent Williamsburg, Norfolk, Jamestown, the College of William & Mary, and each of the more than sixty counties in the colony. Among those who served as burgesses, besides Patrick Henry, were George Washington, Thomas Jefferson, Peyton Randolph, and George Wythe. James Madison and Edmund Randolph also both served in public office for the first time at the Capitol as members of the Virginia Convention. If the House of Burgesses and the Council deadlocked, representatives from each chamber met in the second-floor joint conference room above the piazza—a literal bridge between the upper and lower houses of the legislature.

The Capitol was not only the place where these men strode toward independence but also very much a training ground for those who would create a new, democratically elected representative government—based on a separation of powers that would restrict government's ability to trample the rights of the people. The Speaker's chair in the Hall of the House of Burgesses dates to the 1730s, a silent witness to the creation of this new republic. The government that met in the Capitol did not, of course, establish equality for all. Laws passed here continued to protect the institution of slavery, perpetuated gender inequality, discriminated against free people of color, and displaced American Indians from ancestral homelands.

The first Capitol was completed in 1705 and burned in 1747. After some debate about whether to relocate the seat of government, a second Capitol was completed in 1753. This building incorporated parts of the surviving walls of its predecessor and retained the original layout of the building but differed in appearance. The most notable changes were the squaring off of the projecting apsidal southern ends of both wings and the addition of a two-story portico on its west facade. It was in this second building that revolution and independence were debated.

After Virginia's government moved to Richmond in 1780, the Capitol building was repurposed for a variety of uses, including a ladies' school, a hospital, and a district court. The building gradually fell into disrepair and finally, in 1832, was once again destroyed by fire.

In 1929, Colonial Williamsburg decided to reconstruct the first Capitol because it was more thoroughly documented than the second one. It was built on the foundation of the original building and based on a contemporary engraving of the building discovered in the 1920s. Reconstruction began in 1931, and the building opened to the public in 1934.

The DECLARATION *of* RIGHTS

The Declaration of Rights, adopted at the Capitol on June 12, 1776, expressed many of the sentiments soon to be echoed in Thomas Jefferson's Declaration of Independence—as is clear from its first two clauses:

> That all men are by nature equally free and independent and have certain inherent rights, of which, when they enter into a state of society, they cannot, by any compact, deprive or divest their posterity; namely, the enjoyment of life and liberty, with the means of acquiring and possessing property, and pursuing and obtaining happiness and safety.

> That all power is vested in, and consequently derived from, the people; that magistrates are their trustees and servants and at all times amenable to them.

2 Secretary's Office
Private

Constructed in 1748 after fire destroyed the Capitol the previous year, this one-story brick building served as the office of the secretary of the colony and as a storage facility for public records. It was also a training venue for county court clerks. Appropriately for a fireproof structure, little decorative woodwork was installed on the interior, and the original floor was paved with stone. Despite the potential hazards, four fireplaces were built to provide heat in winter and drive off the damp and mold in summer.

Reflecting the prestige of the office, the building's brickwork, laid in Flemish bond with glazed headers, is of very high quality. The exterior openings and corners are accentuated by rubbed bricks of a uniform orange-red color, a fashion that was popular throughout the Tidewater region in the middle of the eighteenth century.

After the move of the state government to Richmond in 1780, the structure served various uses, including government offices, a grammar school, and a residence. The small graveyard that sits between the Capitol and the Secretary's Office is that of the Jones family, who lived here well into the twentieth century and who had no connection to the building's colonial past. The building was restored in 1939–1940.

3 Palmer House
Private

John Palmer, lawyer and bursar of the College of William & Mary, built this two-story brick house soon after an earlier structure on the site burned in 1754. The plan of the house—two rooms deep with a side passage providing access to a "hall," or entertaining room, in the front and a "chamber," or bedroom, in the rear—was a type that appeared in Williamsburg by the middle of the eighteenth century and later began to be seen in rural areas of Virginia. The holes in the brickwork, known as *putlog holes,* were left when the masons who built the Palmer House removed their scaffolding. A symmetrical pleasure garden is designed around a central sundial. An antebellum addition was removed when the building was restored in 1952.

4 R. Charlton's Coffeehouse
Open to ticket holders

Coffeehouses, known as "penny universities," were a place to exchange the latest discoveries, news, and gossip. Each coffeehouse had its own character, usually strongly influenced by location; in

R. Charlton's Coffeehouse

Virginia the colonists sought to capture some essence of the coffee-house culture of London. Coffeehouses embraced the idea that gentry and tradesmen were all welcome and, as a seventeenth-century broadside put it, may "without affront sit down together." In the case of Charlton's, because of its proximity to the Capitol and a theater, there was likely a lively mixture of elite politicians and lower and middling sorts making a living at playacting. Unlike taverns, coffeehouses didn't offer lodging, but the archaeological record indicates that alcohol was generously served at Charlton's.

As a place for exchanging ideas, the coffeehouse was very much a product of the Enlightenment. Today's guests can exchange ideas with eighteenth-century interpreters while sampling authentic versions of historic "hot liquors": coffee, tea, and chocolate. Note this is an exhibition site not a working coffeehouse; the drinks are just samples.

In October 1765, a crowd gathered nearby to protest the Stamp Act and cornered George Mercer, the chief distributor of stamps in Virginia. Governor Francis Fauquier, who was seated on the porch of the coffeehouse, intervened to avoid violence.

The building that became Charlton's coffeehouse was built in 1749–1750. Richard Charlton, a wigmaker, opened the coffeehouse in the early 1760s. It was frequented by influential figures, including George Washington and Thomas Jefferson. But it was apparently not a financial success since in 1767 Charlton advertised in the *Virginia Gazette* that his coffeehouse was now a tavern. Williamsburg apparently never supported more than one coffeehouse, and none replaced Charlton's.

The building stood until about 1889 when a large Victorian house was built on the site using some of the original foundations, framing members, trim, and even doors, windows, and shutters. That house was relocated to Henry Street, outside the Historic Area, in 1995. The surviving architectural fragments were essential to the design efforts, providing information about the frame, interior and exterior finishes, and even early paint colors.

PEACE PIPES

As part of the research that preceded the reconstruction of Charlton's coffeehouse, archaeologists recovered hundreds of objects from nearby trash deposits. One that stood out was a hand-carved stone pipe.

The pipe, which has a square stem and a large bowl, had a design common to the Cherokees.

Englishmen often encountered Indian pipe rituals during negotiations between colonies and tribes. During the years Charlton operated his coffeehouse, several Indian delegations came to town to discuss Anglo-Indian relations. In April 1762, Governor Fauquier and his council met with the Cherokee headman Outacite and his entourage. An observer recorded that Outacite "first took up his calumet or pipe (which is their most sacred emblem of peace) and after having well lighted it, he then gave to his Honour to take a few wiffs, and to the council in order."

Charlton's coffeehouse was reconstructed in 2008–2009, the first full reconstruction on Duke of Gloucester Street in fifty years. Based on extensive archaeological and architectural research, the reconstructed coffeehouse incorporated much of the foundations of the original building and was built with exact copies of the fragments that survived from the original building. The copies were made using traditional materials and methods.

5 Edinburgh Castle Tavern
Private

Originally built by Francis Sharp circa 1717–1719, this reconstructed building had a plan similar to many of the earliest buildings in Williamsburg, with a small enclosed porch that opened into an entertaining room. Beginning in the 1720s and 1730s, these porches were increasingly seen as old-fashioned and later plans replaced them with central passages. The building was reconstructed in 1942.

6 John Crump House
Private

Originally constructed about 1719 by Francis Sharp as one of Williamsburg's smaller taverns, this building was extended to its present size before the end of the eighteenth century. Henry Wetherburn, one of the town's most successful tavern keepers, bought the establishment in 1742. His nephew Edward Nicholson inherited the property and rented it to various businessmen. John Crump, the town jailer, acquired it in 1789 and continued to operate a tavern through the first decade of the 1800s. Later, the building became so dilapidated that it was condemned and razed at the end of the nineteenth century. Reconstruction in 1941 was based on the archaeological remains of the foundations, insurance plats dating from the ownership of John Crump, and a late nineteenth-century photograph.

7 Nicolson Store
Private

Robert Nicolson, a tailor and merchant, insured a "Wood Store two Story 34 feet by 20 feet" (the size of the present building) on this site in 1796. The structure reflects the standard Virginia store layout of the period. The unheated front salesroom took up most of the first floor with a smaller, heated counting room at the back. The second floor was used as a residence and for storage. Despite the addition of a western extension in the early nineteenth century, the original 1751 building survived enough to guide the restoration of 1949–1950.

Pasteur & Galt Apothecary Shop

8 Shields Tavern
Open to the public
Tavern keeper John Marot probably built the first part of a building in 1707. Within ten years he had extended the structure to the east. In the early 1740s, James Shields, Marot's son-in-law, took over the tavern. Although close to the Capitol, Shields Tavern attracted lower gentry and successful middling customers. The building was lost to fire in 1858. Today, a tavern once again operates on the site.

9 Pasteur & Galt Apothecary Shop
Open to ticket holders
When Dr. William Pasteur and Dr. John Minson Galt became partners in 1775, the *Virginia Gazette* announced that "they intend practising Physic and Surgery to their fullest Extent . . . they intend also . . . to keep full and complete Assortments of Drugs and Medicines, which they will endeavour to procure of the very best in Quality."

The ad gives a sense of the range of services provided by the apothecary, which go well beyond those of a modern pharmacist. Galt also practiced midwifery and was visiting physician to the Public Hospital for Persons of Insane and Disordered Minds in Williamsburg. Both Pasteur and Galt apprenticed in Williamsburg and then studied in London.

In November 1775, Pasteur was elected mayor of Williamsburg. He sold his share of the business to Galt in 1778 to become an oyster merchant. Galt remained in business on the property until his death in 1808.

Pasteur likely built the shop soon after he purchased the property in 1760. Today, in the shop, the reconstruction of which was completed in 1951, copies of Galt's certificates from his London studies are on display along with antique surgical tools, compounding and dispensing equipment, and reproduction splints and dental tools. Original British delft drug jars line one wall. The Latin names on the storage drawers represent ingredients from the site records, including advertisements listing aloes of all sorts, Peruvian bark, and senna. Also displayed are medications compounded from formulas in eighteenth-century professional pharmacy books.

10 Scrivener Store
Private
Merchant Joseph Scrivener bought this property in 1762. He lived in the house and operated a grocery here until he died in 1772. The house was built between 1745 and 1762, torn down in 1906, and

rebuilt in 1941. The reconstruction was based on archaeological excavations, a photograph taken before demolition, and recollections of a neighbor who remembered the original structure.

11 Alexander Craig House
Private

The two-story structure is a composite of various additions made to a small building. It is not clear when it was first built, though the lot was sold "with ye houses thereon" as early as 1712. The two doors at the front of the building suggest that at least in some periods it served as both a dwelling (on one side) and a business (on the other). During the eighteenth century, a wide variety of tradesmen, including a goldsmith, a tavern keeper, a glazier, and a series of wigmakers, owned the property. Saddler Alexander Craig owned it from 1755 until his death in 1776. The section at the right, which was used as a shop, is the oldest portion of the building. The west wing was a late eighteenth-century addition. The property boasts a pleasure garden, an orchard of fruit trees, and pleached arbors. Although the type of business changed a number of times, the shop portion of the house continued to be used for commercial purposes until early in the twentieth century. Before Colonial Williamsburg restored the property in 1941–1942, the eighteenth-century building was still standing but with many alterations, including both vertical and horizontal additions and changes in the windows and doors.

12 John Coke Office
Private

The building that originally stood on this lot may have been built by James Shields, an early owner of the lot along with the tavern next to it. The building's name comes from a pair of insurance policies taken out by John Coke in 1806 and 1809, the first pieces of documentary evidence that make a clear reference to the building. It was reconstructed in 1930 and substantially altered to its present form in 1958 to better reflect its eighteenth-century appearance, including the removal of a shed addition that had been constructed for the convenience of a previous tenant.

13 Alexander Purdie House
Part of the King's Arms Tavern

James Shields likely built a house sometime before 1707 when the property was conveyed to William Byrd. Other owners included merchant James Crosby, merchants Buchanan & Company, and Dr.

Kenneth McKenzie. McKenzie used the main part as his home and the eastern part as a medical office, and his first wife, Mary, may have run a millinery out of the house. The Scottish-born Alexander Purdie, printer and publisher of the *Virginia Gazette,* purchased it in 1767.

No longer standing when Colonial Williamsburg acquired the property in 1927, the structure was reconstructed following archaeological excavations in 1951. The pleasure garden, a simple four-square design, has plants of seasonal interest, including shadblow trees, pomegranates, and oak-leaf hydrangeas. Today, the house serves as the east wing of the King's Arms Tavern, though it was originally a separate building.

14 King's Arms Tavern
Open to the public
Jane Vobe, one of Williamsburg's most successful tavern keepers, ran the King's Arms Tavern, which she renamed the Eagle Tavern after the Revolution. Prior to the construction of the tavern, a storehouse stood on the site above a large brick vaulted cellar. This enormous storage room was fitted out with racks for storing wine and beer. Unfortunately, by the end of the eighteenth century, its arched ceiling had collapsed and the cellar filled in. Reconstructed in 1951, today's King's Arms again operates as a tavern. The modern tavern is much longer than in the eighteenth century, connected as it is to the Alexander Purdie House.

15 Wigmaker (King's Arms Barber Shop)
Open to ticket holders
Those who wore wigs included not only landed gentry like Thomas Jefferson and Patrick Henry but also tradesmen like blacksmith James Anderson, merchants like John Greenhow, tavern keepers, and clergymen. Ladies also wore wigs, but only ladies of the gentry. George Washington chose not to wear one. Only about 5 percent of Williamsburg's population wore wigs.

Workingmen and women also patronized the wigmaker, since in addition to wigs this tradesperson provided barbering and hairdressing services.

Wigmaker Edward Charlton resided in Williamsburg from 1752–1792 and practiced the trades of wig making, barbering, and hairdressing.

The wig shop still today imports hair from Europe, including human, horse, yak, and goat hair. The wigs and hairpieces go on the heads of interpreters. The shop displays samples not only of the hair used to make wigs but also of the pomades and soap made at the shop.

Words from the Wig Shop

- **Blockhead**—A piece of elm or ash carved to the size and shape of a customer's head, allowing wigmakers to ensure a perfect fit.

- **Powder Room**—A small room where ladies and gentleman went to powder their wigs.

- **Wig**—A shortened version of periwig, which was derived from the French *perruque*.

Sound Familiar? A *blockhead*—a head with no intelligence in it— was an insult, even in the eighteenth century. And a *bigwig* denoted importance since prominent men often wore large hairpieces.

Anthony Geoghegan is thought to have established a business as a wigmaker and barber in a shop on this site in 1768 while the property was held by Jane Vobe, tavern keeper. It was reconstructed in 1951.

16 Charlton House
Private
The brick foundations and cellar of a smaller building were incorporated into the Charlton House, which was built sometime before 1772, the year Edward Charlton bought the property. Charlton was a wigmaker and barber. During the nineteenth century, the rear portion was taken down to ground level and various additions were made to the back of the house. The rear half was reconstructed in 1929–1930.

17 Raleigh Tavern
Open to ticket holders
The Raleigh Tavern, which was named for Sir Walter Raleigh, who attempted the first colonization of Virginia, was the site of many crucial political discussions, in part due to its size and location near the Capitol and in part because of its standing as one of the finest taverns in Virginia. In the spring of 1774, after Royal Governor Lord Dunmore dissolved the House of Burgesses for objecting to the closing of Boston's port after its Tea Party, eighty-nine burgesses reconvened for an unofficial meeting at the Raleigh. There they formed an association committed to not importing British goods and called for a meeting of representatives from all the colonies. The meeting they called for became the Continental Congress that met in Philadelphia and that eventually passed the Declaration of Independence.

The Raleigh was also the site of social and cultural gatherings. Large private rooms like the Apollo Room could be rented out for balls, lectures, concerts, meetings, dinners, or gaming—including gambling. Cards, backgammon, and billiards were especially popular.

Tavern customers were predominantly male, but Williamsburg taverns occasionally served women. Both men and women were tavern keepers, and workers were both black and white, enslaved and free.

Like all taverns, the Raleigh offered food and lodging. The public lodging rooms were certainly uncomfortable by modern standards: not only did customers have to share a room with strangers but often they had to share a bed and even sleep on the floor.

Established in the 1710s, the tavern grew in size and reputation through the colonial period. The original two-room structure was constructed around 1710. It was expanded to the east in 1733, when a semi-enclosed porch was added, similar to the one at the Edinburgh

LOVESTRUCK

Painted in gold above the mantel of the Raleigh's Apollo Room are Latin words that translate to "Jollity, the offspring of wisdom and good living." The Apollo Room often provided jollity but not, alas, for a young Thomas Jefferson. While a student at the College of William & Mary in 1763, Jefferson attended a ball where he danced with Rebecca Burwell, whom he called Belinda and with whom he was much infatuated. He described the scene in a letter to a friend:

> Last night, as merry as agreeable company and dancing with Belinda in the Apollo could make me, I never could have thought the succeeding sun would have seen me so wretched as I now am! I was prepared to say a great deal: I had dressed up in my own mind, such thoughts as occurred to me, in as moving language as I knew how, and expected to have performed in a tolerably creditable manner. But, good God! When I had an opportunity of venting them, a few broken sentences, uttered in great disorder, and interrupted with pauses of uncommon length, were the too visible marks of my strange confusion!

Castle Tavern further east along Duke of Gloucester Street. Around 1750, two formal entertaining spaces, the Daphne and Apollo Rooms, were added in the rear. Sometime before 1773, an open porch was added facing Duke of Gloucester Street.

The tavern burned down in 1859. Fortunately, elements of the exterior of the building and an interior view of the Apollo Room were included in 1848 drawings by Benson Lossing, who traveled around the country visiting important Revolutionary sites.

When the restoration of Williamsburg began in 1926, two modern brick stores stood on the site of the Raleigh. The reconstruction, between 1929 and 1932, was also aided by early insurance policies and archaeological excavations that revealed most of the original foundations. The reconstructed Raleigh was Colonial Williamsburg's first exhibition building. It was initially completed without its late colonial porch, which scholars then believed to postdate the Revolution. But after archaeology and further documentary research confirmed that it was in place before 1773, the porch was reconstructed in 2017.

18 Raleigh Tavern Bakery (Raleigh Tavern Kitchen)
Open to the public
This large reconstructed kitchen, behind the tavern, represents the space where meals for tavern guests were prepared. Today, the building houses the Raleigh Tavern Bakery, which serves light refreshments.

19 The Unicorn's Horn and John Carter's Store
Private
Two brothers, Dr. James Carter and Dr. William Carter, used the west portion of a building built in 1765 as an apothecary shop under the sign of the unicorn's horn. The unicorn's horn was a symbol of an apothecary based on the myth that unicorn horns held healing powers. A third brother, John Carter, ran a general store in the other half of the building and also lived there with his family. The building burned down in 1859. Colonial Williamsburg excavated the site in 1931 and completed its reconstruction in 1953.

20 Silversmith (The Golden Ball)
Trade shop open to ticket holders; store open to the public
London-trained jeweler and silversmith James Craig located his business at this site in 1765. In 1772 Craig began advertising his shop as "the Golden Ball," a name commonly used by jewelers and goldsmiths. Here he lived and worked with his family of five and at least one slave until his death in 1793.

The first building on this site was a tavern built in 1724. Craig extended the building by six feet into a passage between his shop and the newly built Carter store next door. That building survived until 1907. It was reconstructed in 1948.

Today, one side of the Golden Ball houses the silversmiths and engravers who, using eighteenth-century techniques, practice and preserve the trades of hollowware, flatware, and jewelry making. The other side of the building is a retail jewelry store where some of the work made by the tradespeople is available.

The ALCHEMIST

The London Tradesman was published in 1747 to help youths choose a suitable profession. Here is part of what the *Tradesman* had to say about silversmiths.

> The goldsmith, or as some call him, silversmith, is employed in making all manner of Utensils in those rich metals, either for ornament or use....
>
> ...He must be conversant in alchemy; that is, in all the properties of metals: He must know...the various Methods of extracting and refining them...the secret of mixing them with their proper alloy...and distinguishing the real from the fictitious.
>
> From hence, it must be conjectured that he ought to be possessed of a solid Judgment as well as a mechanical hand and head.

21 Milliner (Margaret Hunter Shop)
Open to ticket holders

Millinery shops were retail and social spaces, catering to both men and women of all levels of society. While today's milliners focus on hats, the eighteenth-century milliner made a much greater variety of fashionable accessories and clothing items, including shifts, shirts, aprons, cloaks, ruffles, and neck stocks. These were often preferred to the imported items also available on her shelves. Many milliners were additionally trained in other branches of the fashion trades, like mantua making (dressmaking), quilting, embroidery, and fan making, all of which continue to be practiced in today's shop.

Millinery was one of the few trades dominated by women. This shop was owned and operated by Margaret Hunter, one of five milliners in the city prior to the Revolution. By the 1780s, five enslaved individuals—Will, Agga, Milly, Sall, and Jenny—also lived on the property and assisted in the running of the business. One of the women was trained in clearstarching and ironing, possibly providing a fine laundry service on-site.

Typical of commercial buildings, this shop has a gable-end facade and an interior divided between a storefront with shelves and a smaller counting office with a fireplace in the rear. Probably built by Harmer and King, merchants, who occupied the site until 1746, the building was later used by the physician-apothecary George Gilmer. Hunter rented and then purchased the shop shortly after 1770. The building was a filling station and garage when restoration began in 1930.

22 Liberty Lounge (Margaret Hunter Workshop)
Open to ticketed members of the military
For ticketed active-duty, veteran, and retired military and their families, Liberty Lounge, just behind the milliner, offers a relaxing respite. Amenities include free Wi-Fi, complimentary hot and cold drinks, and coloring sheets and crayons and a large chalkboard for kids. Guests need a blue star sticker, which they can get at any Colonial Williamsburg ticket location.

23 Russell House
Private
Named after a family who lived here in the eighteenth century, this residence was built by 1745, modified with a rear addition and a cellar by 1776, likely razed by 1815, and reconstructed in 1949.

24 Prentis House
Private
The Prentis family owned the residence built sometime before 1725 and expanded by 1765 for much of the eighteenth century. The pleasure garden at the house features a small orchard balanced by the stable and paddock at the rear of the site. The house burned to the ground in 1842 and was reconstructed in 1938.

25 Wetherburn's Tavern
Open to ticket holders
This structure is one of the most thoroughly documented buildings in Williamsburg—architecturally, archaeologically, and historically.

Henry Wetherburn erected the original, eastern portion of the building in the 1730s. With business thriving, he added the west extension with a large fashionable entertaining room by 1752. This "great room" occasionally served as an informal town hall in which scientific lectures, political gatherings, and balls took place.

The tavern depended on twelve enslaved men and women to cook, serve, clean, tend the garden, and groom customers' horses. They

WETHERBURN

lived in the attics over the kitchen and stable.

Behind the kitchen and adjacent buildings is a simple square kitchen garden filled with herbs and vegetables of the period.

The building was restored in 1966–1967, when interior partitions and windows and doors were returned to their original locations based on close examination of the surviving structure. A room-by-room probate inventory, taken just a month after Wetherburn's death in 1760, was used to refurnish the tavern. In the rear yard, the dairy survives with its original framing, though the other outbuildings were reconstructed on their eighteenth-century foundations. The exterior has been painted off-white, reflecting recent reconsideration of the tavern's surviving paint.

26 Tarpley's Store
Open to the public

James Tarpley bought this lot from Henry Wetherburn in 1759. He erected and operated a retail store at this location until his death in 1764. Over the years, Tarpley had various business partners, including John Thompson after 1761. The building, reconstructed in 1937, is once again a mercantile establishment, operating as Tarpley, Thompson & Company.

Waller Street

27, 28 Benjamin Powell House and Office
Open for special programs only

Benjamin Powell, a successful builder, bought this house and property in 1763 from Benjamin Waller, a prominent local lawyer and owner of much of the land east of the Capitol. Powell sold the house in 1782, and it changed hands several times before Benjamin Carter Waller, son of the early owner, bought it in 1794. The front frame portion of the house was added before 1782 to the original brick house that lies behind facing south. The small brick building next to the larger house probably served as the office of Benjamin Carter Waller's son, Dr. Robert Waller. The kitchen was built between 1820 and 1840 while the smokehouse and dairy may be slightly earlier. During the house's restoration in 1955–1956, everything above the present eaves level was reconstructed. The kitchen garden contains an assortment of fruits, vegetables, and herbs reflecting a colonial diet. The house is open for special programming for Colonial Williamsburg, including escorted school groups.

29 Elizabeth Carlos House
Private

In 1772 Elizabeth Carlos bought this lot with a one-story frame house. Like many small houses of the period, it did not survive into the twentieth century but was reconstructed in 1957. A pleasure garden was planted, probably around the same time, in a typical four-square pattern using a wellhead as a focal point. Its deep brown color, so common in the period for modest houses, would have been familiar to early residents. Carlos was a milliner and dressmaker who carried on her business in her home.

30 Christiana Campbell's Tavern
Open to the public

Christiana Campbell announced in October 1771 that she had opened a "TAVERN in the House, behind the Capitol" where she promised "genteel Accommodations, and the very best Entertainment," by which she meant food and drink. Her distinguished clientele included George Washington. He recorded in his diary that, when he came to town to attend the House of Burgesses in 1772, he dined here ten times within two months. The building was reconstructed in 1954–1956. The focal point in the shade garden next to the tavern is the native yaupon holly. Today, Christiana Campbell's Tavern again entertains guests with food and drink.

31 The Blue Bell
Private

Little is known about this site, which probably had a building on it around 1707. At various times, the Blue Bell (the name was mentioned in a 1770 letter) housed a tavern, a lodging house, a store, and a gunsmith's shop. After archaeological excavations in 1932 and 1946, Colonial Williamsburg reconstructed the building in 1952.

32 Powell's Tenement
Private

In the eighteenth century, there was a house and shop on this site. Wheelwright and riding chair maker Peter Powell rented a shop here from 1755 to about 1770. The building was reconstructed in 1934.

33 Presbyterian Meetinghouse (George Davenport Stable)
Open to ticket holders

Presbyterians began worshipping in 1765 in a building on George Davenport's property. Besides Bruton Parish Church, this was the only authorized place of worship in Williamsburg before the Revolution. Dissenters from the Church of England, like Presbyterians and Baptists, were instrumental to the passage in 1786 of the Virginia Statute for Religious Freedom. That bill was originally drafted by Thomas Jefferson in 1777. The building was reconstructed in 1950.

34 Isham Goddin Shop
Private

Militiaman Isham Goddin acquired a small shop on this site in 1778 for two hundred pounds. The building was reconstructed in 1954 and now serves as a hotel accommodation.

35, 36 David Morton House and Shop
Private

Tailor David Morton purchased this lot in 1777. The garden, based partly on a 1782 map and partly on archaeological excavations, features a wellhead as a central focal point. The house was reconstructed in 1953 and today is a hotel facility.

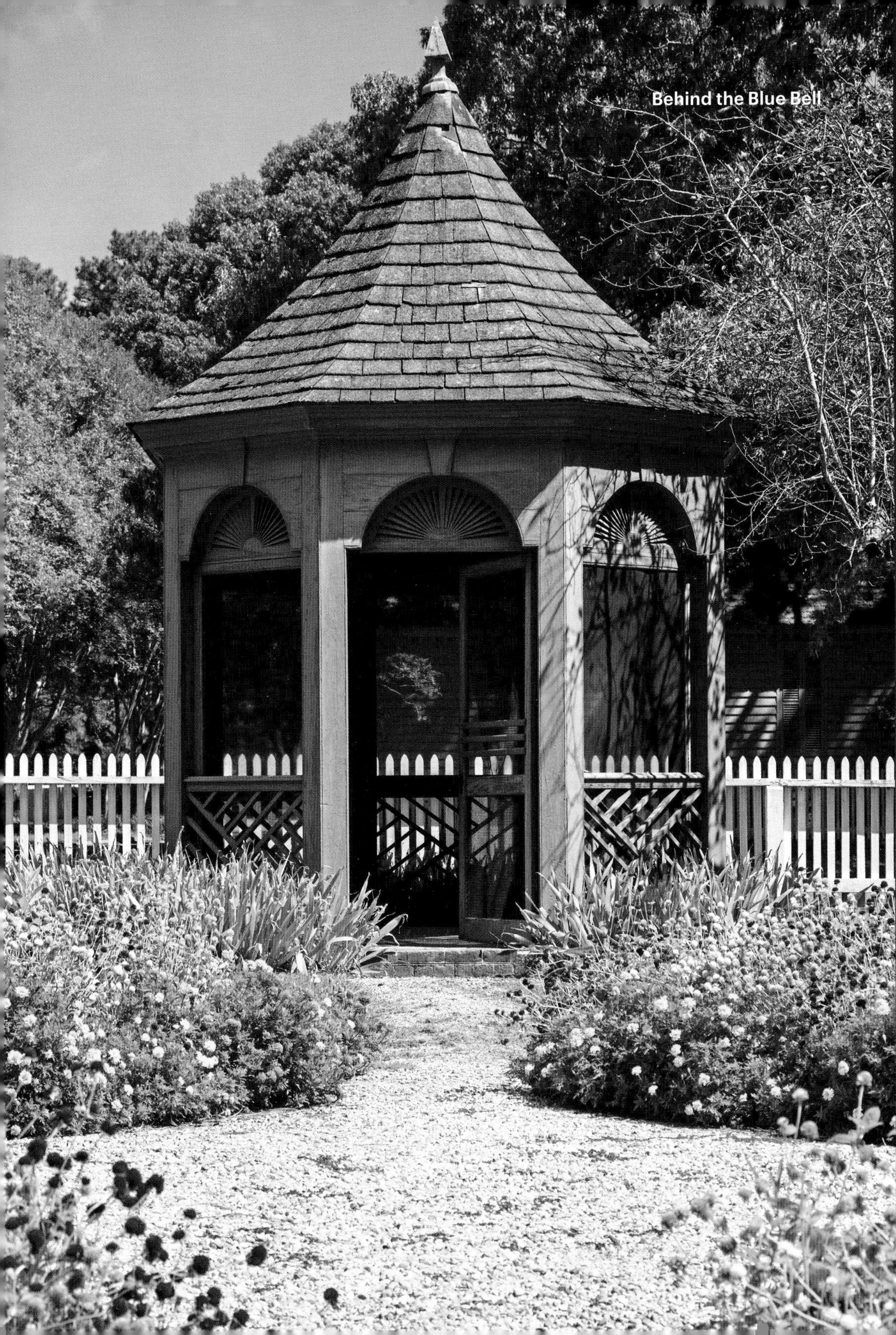
Behind the Blue Bell

York Street

37 George Jackson House and Store
Private

This property was once owned by a merchant who risked his life as well as his fortune during the Revolutionary War. George Jackson chartered a ship, sailed it to Bermuda, and returned with a supply of much-needed gunpowder for the American forces. Jackson acquired the property shortly after he moved to Williamsburg from Norfolk in 1773 or 1774. The different roof slopes reflect the building's evolution in at least two distinct phases, with the shop in the east half and the house in the west. The arrangement of the windows and door of the east wing are typical of shops in the eighteenth century. Reconstructed in 1954, the property now serves as hotel accommodations.

38 Cogar Shop
Private

This small eighteenth-century building was moved from King and Queen County, Virginia, to this lot in 1947. Colonial Williamsburg acquired it in 1964.

39 Robert Nicolson House
Private

Robert Nicolson, a tailor and merchant, built this gambrel-roofed house. The off-center entrance door testifies to two periods of construction, with the eastern part built in the early 1750s and the western part added to accommodate his growing family around 1766. It was restored in 1940 as a private residence.

Francis Street

40 Benjamin Waller House
Private

Benjamin Waller acquired this lot before 1750. A prominent Williamsburg attorney, Waller was George Wythe's teacher. He held a variety of offices: burgess, city recorder, clerk of the General Court, judge of the Court of Admiralty, and vestryman of Bruton Parish. Waller probably used the office, which is adjacent to the house on the east, as a clerk's office for his many posts and also for his private law practice.

The smokehouse is an original structure. Like many old houses, this one is the product of several building phases. The earliest portion, the single room to the left of the front door, dates to about 1750. The building was extended to the west in the 1760s and achieved its present form, including a long rear wing, by 1782. The house and outbuildings were restored between 1951 and 1953.

41 Bassett Hall
Open to ticket holders
When John D. Rockefeller Jr. and Abby Aldrich Rockefeller came to Williamsburg during the restoration of the town, they lived in this eighteenth-century frame house. Today the house and grounds look much as they did when the Rockefellers lived here.

The Bray family owned the property from the early seventeenth century until 1753 when it was transferred to Philip Johnson, husband of Elizabeth Bray. Johnson probably built the present house soon after. From 1796 to 1839, Burwell Bassett, a Virginia legislator and the nephew of Martha Washington, owned the property.

The Rockefellers acquired Bassett Hall in 1927, though they didn't move in until several years later. The restoration of the house began in 1928. The Rockefellers oversaw the work and also planned the interior decoration, drawing on their many interests in the arts: Chinese porcelain, Oriental carpets, European tapestries, and modern American art. Abby Aldrich Rockefeller also had an exceptional collection of early American folk art. Outside, the Rockefellers realigned the outbuildings (smokehouse, kitchen, and dairy) near the house to allow for a better view of the property, and they landscaped fourteen acres of gardens.

Rockefeller family members presented the property to Colonial Williamsburg in 1978, and a year later the John D. Rockefeller 3rd Fund gave the furnishings to the Foundation. A complete restoration of the Bassett Hall complex, including the gardens and the historic interiors, was undertaken in 2000–2002.

42 George Davenport House
Private
George Davenport and his descendants owned this property until 1779 when it was sold to John Draper, a blacksmith who had come to Virginia with Royal Governor Lord Botetourt. It was reconstructed in 1950.

43, 44 James Moir House and Shop
Private
This house is named for the tailor who owned this property from 1777 to about 1800. In 1784, when a grammar school was established in the old Capitol, Moir advertised that he had furnished his house to accommodate eight or ten pupils and would lodge, board, and wash and mend for them at a low price. Moir operated his business in an adjoining shop. Both the house and the shop were reconstructed in 1952.

45 Gunsmith (Ayscough House)
Open to ticket holders
At the Ayscough House, gunsmiths make and repair rifles, fowling pieces, and pistols using eighteenth-century-style tools and technology. Gunsmiths then and now had to be able to forge iron from a bar, cast brass or silver from scrap, and stock a gun from wood.

The WEAPON *that* WON INDEPENDENCE

At the Colonial Williamsburg Musket Range, you can fire live rounds at a target using two reproduction flintlock firearms. Even those familiar with modern firearms will find these weapons have a different feel.

Certified instructors provide guidance on how to handle and operate a second-model brown Bess, or short land service pattern musket—a service weapon used by British and American soldiers during the war. A replica of a fowling piece, a precursor to the modern shotgun that was the most popular firearm in North America, is also available to try. It was used for hunting and farm pest control.

Must be age fourteen or older to participate. Guests younger than seventeen must be accompanied by a legally responsible adult who is not shooting. Shuttle transportation is required; participants may not drive themselves to the range.

Williamsburg's gunsmiths' inventories and advertisements reflect this broad range of skills. John Brush's inventory from 1726 included "New Cast brass" and melting pots as well as 172 pounds of old brass. William Geddy advertised that he could provide "Gun Work, such as Guns and Pistols Stocks, plain or neatly varnished, Locks and Mountings, Barrels blued, bored, and rifled." And William Willis's ad "informs the publick that he . . . intends to carry on his business in all its branches." When Willis moved to Norfolk, he established his shop "at the Sign of the *Cross Guns*." Today's gunsmiths carry on the trade in all its branches at the sign of the crossed guns near the Capitol.

The house was purchased by Christopher Ayscough, a former gardener, and his wife, Anne, who had been the head cook for Lieutenant Governor Francis Fauquier at the Palace. They established a tavern on the site in 1768, which probably stood west of the present structure. The funds probably came from a bequest of £150 that Fauquier left Anne "in recompence of her great fidelity and attention to me in all my Illness, and of the great Economy with which she conducted the Expenses of my kitchen during my residence at Williamsburg." The Ayscoughs' tavern-keeping venture was short-lived. A succession of commercial establishments occupied the building in the eighteenth century. A large shop window and the gable-end entrance attest to the structure's early commercial use.

Original framing was revealed during the 1932 restoration. The shed at the rear was a late eighteenth-century addition.

46, 47 William Finnie House and Quarters
Private

This house was probably built around 1770 by William Pasteur, one of the town's leading apothecaries. Called "the handsomest house in town" by St. George Tucker in 1809, it was a precursor of the neoclassicism that began to transform American architectural tastes after the Revolution. The two-story central block, with its pedimented gable and flanking one-story wings, gained currency in Virginia and neighboring states in the following decades. From the 1770s to the mid-1780s, Colonel William Finnie, quartermaster general of the Southern Department during the Revolution, and his family lived here. This largely original house was restored in 1932, with further work completed in 1952. The small building just east of the house is known as the William Finnie Quarters and is also an original structure.

48 Nelson-Galt Office
Private

This small office near the Nelson-Galt House is original. In the eigh-teenth century, the word *office* described any outbuilding whose use was not otherwise designated.

49, 50 Nelson-Galt House and Kitchen
Private

The house is the oldest dwelling in town and one of the oldest houses in Virginia. The framing members encased in the central part of the present house date to 1695. The chimneys and flanking shed closets are later additions probably made when William Robertson, clerk of the Council, bought the property and remodeled the house about 1709. Thomas Nelson Jr. owned the house later in the century. Nelson signed the Declaration of Independence, commanded Virginia's forces during the Yorktown campaign, and succeeded Thomas Jeffer-son as governor of the Commonwealth of Virginia. Dr. Alexander Dickie Galt purchased the house in 1823. The house was restored and the kitchen reconstructed in 1951–1952.

51 Shields Stable
Private

The rough appearance of this unpainted stable is typical of many agri-cultural and domestic outbuildings of colonial Virginia. It was built in 1953.

52 Chiswell-Bucktrout House
Private

Accused of killing Robert Rutledge during a tavern brawl, Colonel John Chiswell was arrested for murder in 1766. Bail was refused, but three of Chiswell's friends, who were judges of the General Court, reversed the decision and released him on bail. Many Virginians attributed this leniency to Chiswell's political and family connections. He died in October 1766 on the day before his trial—by his own hand, it was rumored. A study of structural timbers in a fragment of the house that survived into the twentieth century provided the evidence for the 1951 reconstruction of this elongated hipped-roof dwelling. Today, the house and its freestanding kitchen are hotel facilities.

48

Nicholson Street

53 Coke-Garrett House
Private

This long, rambling house is made up of three sections. In 1755, John Coke, a goldsmith and tavern keeper, bought the two lots on which the one-story west section stands. He probably built that section in the late 1750s or early 1760s. The Garrett family acquired the property in 1810 and owned it for well over a century. The two-story center portion was built in 1836–1837, and the one-story east section, an eighteenth-century structure, was moved to this site from an unknown location around the same time. The brick office on the far right dates from about 1810. The subdued Greek Revival architecture of the center section merges easily with the colonial styles of the east and west wings. The restoration of the house was carried out in stages from 1928 through 1961. The Chinese-style railing on the west entrance porch duplicates the dilapidated original that was still in place before the restoration.

54 Public Gaol
Open to ticket holders

In a city where the principles of liberty were very publicly developed and debated, perhaps no building represents the conflicted meanings of that word more than the Public Gaol (historically spelled "gaol" instead of "jail"). In 1718, fifteen men who had sailed with Edward Teach, otherwise known as Blackbeard, were held here prior to standing trial for piracy. Of those fifteen, fourteen were hanged after their crewmate Israel Hands testified against them. Hands was pardoned and escaped the gallows.

In addition to hanging, punishments for criminals found guilty included branding, whipping, or standing in the pillory rather than being imprisoned for lengthy sentences. Captured runaway slaves were also held in the gaol before being returned to their owners, usually after being whipped. Other prisoners included ministers who refused to preach in accordance with the laws that favored the Church of England. Financial debtors and people with mental disorders whose families couldn't care for them would be kept in the gaol as well, but under less harsh conditions.

During the Revolution, loyal subjects of the king were frequently jailed alongside accused spies and prisoners of war. Often, the only offense committed by the Loyalists was that they refused to support the cause of American independence.

The initial structure was completed in 1703 and enlarged three times in the colonial period. The building continued to be used as a jail until 1910. Two of the criminal cells and one of the debtors' cells are original, while the rest of the building was reconstructed in 1936.

55 Booker Tenement
Private

This small one-story house is typical of a Williamsburg house of the middling sort of the post-Revolutionary period. An analysis of the tree growth rings in its timbers showed that the wood was cut in 1823–1824. Richard Booker, carpenter and town constable, had begun to rent out rooms here by the spring of 1826.

56 William Randolph Lodgings
Private

This small rental property is unusually short in depth—only twelve feet (and forty-six feet wide). The building was rented in 1735 to William Randolph, the uncle of Peyton Randolph. A burgess and later a councillor, William apparently considered this modest structure an appropriate residence when he came to Williamsburg on government business. It was reconstructed in 1949.

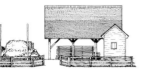

57 Carpenter's Yard
Open to ticket holders

Carpenters built the city of Williamsburg, and they continue to reconstruct and repair buildings using eighteenth-century tools and techniques.

Many carpenters built successful businesses in Williamsburg and became master tradesmen, employing journeymen and apprentices. Enslaved workmen supported the building trades by sawing planks, hewing timbers, and splitting shingles, and many were trained in the more skilled trades of carpentry and joinery, bricklaying and plastering, glazing and house painting.

Among the most successful carpenters in Williamsburg were Benjamin Powell and Philip Moody, both of whom did work for the Commonwealth of Virginia during the Revolutionary War, including building barracks, a hospital for troops, and a stable for cavalry units. Powell was the "undertaker," the colonial-era term for a general contractor, for the Public Hospital.

James Wray's carpenter's yard on Prince George Street near the College of William & Mary was excavated in 2002. Archaeological findings, including sawpits, a workshop, and tools have been enormously useful to historians of the trade.

Carpenters continue to work throughout the Historic Area but can more routinely be found at the Carpenter's Yard on Nicholson Street.

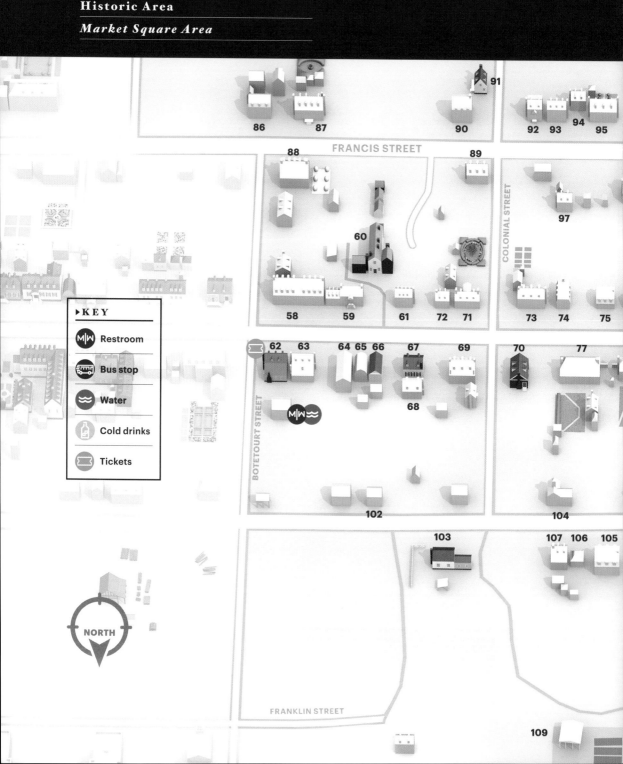

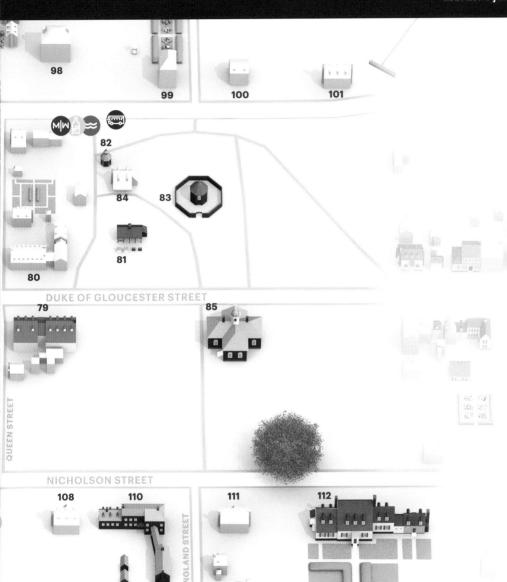

98

99

100

101

M|W

82

84

83

81

80

DUKE OF GLOUCESTER STREET

79

85

QUEEN STREET

NICHOLSON STREET

108

110

111

112

NORTH ENGLAND STREET

Path to Visitor Center,
Great Hopes (113),
Windmill (114), bus stop,
water, and cold drinks

Colonial Williamsburg: The Guide

Blacksmith

Duke of Gloucester Street

58 Brick House Tavern
Private

This lodging house was built as a two-story, six-unit rental property in the early 1760s, but it was reconstructed as just one story. Itinerant tradesmen and others with services or goods to sell would live and work here, advertising their presence in the *Virginia Gazette*. Among those who did so were a surgeon, a jeweler, a watch repairer, a milliner, and a wigmaker. Reconstructed in 1939, it is a hotel facility today, as is the Brick House Tavern Shop behind it.

59 James Anderson House
Private

This site served at various times as a residence and place of business for a tavern keeper, a milliner, a barber and wigmaker, and a chandler and soap boiler before James Anderson purchased the property in 1770. During the Revolution, Anderson operated a public armory behind his home.

60 James Anderson's Blacksmith Shop and Public Armoury
Open to ticket holders

James Anderson's Blacksmith Shop and Public Armoury is a reconstruction of a manufacturing complex that served Virginia as an arms repair facility and metal manufactory during the Revolution. This important, busy complex employed forty men in 1780.

James Anderson began his career as a blacksmith, probably by apprenticing to his uncle. Anderson was successful at the trade and was appointed armorer to the magazine. In that role, he was responsible for the upkeep of Virginia's military arms and equipment stored at the magazine and Governor's Palace. In 1770, Anderson acquired the property where the armory complex presently stands. With the approach of the Revolution, he became armorer for the Committee of Safety, and later for the Commonwealth of Virginia. In 1778, the commonwealth funded an expansion of Anderson's business, enabling the construction of the large armory with its four forges.

Today the complex includes a blacksmith and armorer's workshop, a tin shop, a kitchen, and a workshop for leatherworking. (The leatherworker is in the Magazine from November to April.)

Blacksmiths primarily work with iron and steel. They heat and soften the metal in coal-fired forges, then shape it with a hammer and anvil, and finish and assemble items using a vise, files, and saws. Blacksmiths usually made and repaired hardware, household utensils, vehicle hardware, and agricultural implements. At the armory, the work expanded to include government arms repair, maintenance of ironwork on Williamsburg's public buildings, hardware needed at the state shipyard, fabricating shackles and shackling prisoners in the gaol, and even winding the Capitol clock.

During the war, the tin shop provided tinware for use by Virginia militia and Continental soldiers. Tin was lightweight, strong, and relatively inexpensive and was used to manufacture military accoutrements such as camp kettles, plates, cups, saucepans, shot canisters, lanterns, speaking trumpets (which were used to project voices over long distances), and other sheet-metal wares.

The reconstruction of the armory drew on extensive research by archaeologists, architectural historians, and tradespeople. The design of the principal work building was based on its archaeological remains, comparable trade sites in England and America, and the account books of Anderson and others. The reconstructed complex opened in 2013.

61 Mary Stith House
Private
Mary Stith was the daughter of William Stith, who was president of the College of William & Mary from 1752 to 1755. In her 1813 will, she left this lot, its buildings, and much of her estate to her former slaves. One of the buildings on the lot became part of the armory complex during the Revolution and is today the reconstructed tin shop. The brick building at the front of the property was reconstructed in 1940.

62 William Pitt Store
Open to the public
With enormous shop windows facing Duke of Gloucester Street, the apothecary shop of Robert Davidson, who was mayor of Williamsburg in 1738, once stood on this site. Reconstructed in 1934, this building now houses a gift shop with products for children.

63 William Waters House
Private
This house is named for a wealthy planter from the Eastern Shore who bought the property when he moved to Williamsburg about 1750. It was reconstructed in 1942.

William Pitt Store

64 Waters Storehouse
Private

By 1760, a storehouse was located on this site. This structure and the next two form a fine collection of reconstructed eighteenth-century commercial properties, all of which are oriented with their gable ends to the street. Completed in 1934, Waters Storehouse was the first of the three to be reconstructed.

65 Holt's Storehouse
Private

The three sugar loaves hanging outside the building are the traditional sign of the grocer. John Holt also sold dry goods and china. The store was reconstructed in 1953.

66 M. Dubois Grocer (Hunter's Store)
Open to the public

Tenant grocer M. Dubois conducted business here in the late 1770s. Reconstructed in 1956, the store today carries sweet treats and drinks.

67 Printer and Bookbinder (Printing Office and Post Office)
Open to ticket holders

In the 1750s and 1760s the building on this site served as a post office and a printing office. Pictured on the sign is a post horn, the instrument commonly carried by post riders to announce their arrival.

In the lower level of the building, you can watch newspapers and other printed pieces come off an eighteenth-century-style press. You can also see the leather balls that are used to "beat" ink onto the letters and the cases that hold the type (the upper case holds the capital letters, the lower case holds the small letters).

William Parks set up Williamsburg's first press in 1730 and six years later started Virginia's first newspaper, the *Virginia Gazette*. The *Virginia Gazette* was the official newspaper of Virginia, printed in Williamsburg from 1736 until 1780, when the capital moved to Richmond. Starting in 1766, there were two, and from early 1775 to early 1776 three, competing newspapers in Williamsburg—all called the *Virginia Gazette*. One of those *Gazettes* was printed by William Rind, whose wife, Clementina, took over after his death.

In the upper level of the building, at the bookbindery, pages received from the printer are folded and then beaten with a heavy hammer to make the sheets lie flat. Then the bookbinder stitches them together with linen thread. The covers of better books are made of fine leather decorated with impressed designs with gold leaf.

While excavating the site of Parks's shop, archaeologists uncovered lead border ornaments used in printing paper money during the French and Indian War, bookbinder ornaments, and hundreds of pieces of type. The Printing Office and Post Office building was reconstructed in 1958.

68 Printing Office Workshop
Private

Across the courtyard from the printing office, this building was reconstructed in 1958.

69 George Pitt House
Private

Although built as a residence, this house (on Colonial Street, just off Duke of Gloucester Street) sometimes served as a combination shop and dwelling in the eighteenth century. Dr. George Pitt had an apothecary shop, the Sign of the Rhinoceros, in part of it. The house and its associated outbuildings were all reconstructed in 1936.

Printer

70 Prentis Store
Open to the public

In this classic example of store architecture, the firm of Prentis and Company operated a highly successful business from 1740 until the Revolution. The building is long and narrow, and its gable end faces the street. Through the door above, merchandise could easily be lifted into the loft. Sizable windows that flank the front doorway throw light into the sales space. Windows along the sides were located toward the rear of the building to light the counting room and to leave long, blank walls for ample shelving in the retail room at the front. Built in 1738, the building was used as an automobile service station in the early twentieth century. It was initially restored in 1928–1931. In 1972, after new evidence was discovered, the porch design was changed to accommodate a single side stair, and the cellar cap was rebuilt. Today's Prentis Store offers handcrafted items made by Colonial Williamsburg tradespeople.

71, 72 Orlando Jones House and Office
Private

Born in 1681, Orlando Jones was the grandfather of Martha Dandridge Custis, who married George Washington. The garden features boxwood topiary and seasonal flower beds. The house, office, and kitchen, all reconstructed in 1940, are now hotel accommodations.

73 George Reid House
Private

The original house was probably built around 1740 by George Orr, a blacksmith. George Reid, a merchant who operated a store near the Capitol, enlarged the house ten feet to the west and moved it twelve feet forward around 1790. It was restored in 1934. The kitchen garden has heirloom flowers, vegetables, herbs, and an orchard with heirloom fruit trees.

75, 74 William Lightfoot House and Kitchen
Private

William Lightfoot, a planter, merchant, and attorney, probably built this town house between 1733 and 1740. The reconstructed entrance steps and landing are based on evidence from the original foundation excavated beneath. Two of the exterior shutters are early and served as models for the others. Shutters with fixed louvers appear to have come into common usage at the end of the eighteenth century. They allow air circulation and, even when closed, still allow some light. The house was restored in 1931. The kitchen was reconstructed in 1948–1949.

76 Peter Hay's Shop
Private

In April 1756, the *Maryland Gazette* reported a fire that broke out in this shop and "in less than Half an Hour entirely consumed the same." Fortunately, "the Assistance of a Fire Engine" prevented damage to nearby buildings. The kitchen behind the shop is now a hotel facility. Both were reconstructed in 1952.

77 Ludwell-Paradise House
Private

Although an earlier structure existed on this site, Philip Ludwell III built this elegant two-story brick house as a rental property in 1752–1753. In the 1760s and 1770s, William Rind—and later his widow,

Clementina—operated a press on the premises. The Ludwell-Paradise House was the first property John D. Rockefeller Jr. purchased for the restoration of Williamsburg. When it was restored in 1931, the entrance steps, still outlined against the exterior cellar wall, resumed their original double flight configuration. At the same time, the arches and sills of the first-floor windows were raised to their original positions, which could be easily discerned in the rubbed and gauged brickwork that originally framed them. Basement window grilles were also returned to their original form.

78 The Red Lion
Private

The Red Lion suffered many failures as a tavern, perhaps because other taverns were more convenient to the Capitol. The building was reconstructed in 1939 with a refined brick exterior.

79 Chowning's Tavern
Open to the public

The oldest part of Chowning's was originally built about 1750. In 1766, Josiah Chowning advertised the opening of a tavern where all "may depend upon the best of entertainment for themselves, servants, and horses." Today, Chowning's Tavern again serves food and drink. It was reconstructed in 1941 to reflect its evolution from a pair of separate structures, one a house and one a store, that were joined by a short connector in between them.

80 Market Square Tavern
Private

John Dixon leased this site from the city in 1749 and built a store on it by 1751, the core of which survives just to the east of the main door with its porch. Ten years later, Robert Lyon doubled the size of the building, adding a passage behind the main entrance and two new rooms to the west. Thomas Craig, a later tenant, began to operate it as a public house in 1767. Thomas Jefferson rented rooms here while he studied law. In 1771, Gabriel Maupin bought the building, added nine feet to the east of the original store, and made various improvements. Maupin ran a saddler and harness-making business in the buildings at the back of his property. When the building was restored in 1931–1932, the second floor was removed. Today Market Square Tavern and the Market Square Tavern kitchen are hotel facilities.

81 Market House
Open to the public

In the eighteenth century, vendors at the Williamsburg market house sold butchered livestock, seafood, cheese, eggs, vegetables, fruit, baked goods, and other foods as well as hay, baskets, and other supplies. Customers included housewives, servants, slaves, and visitors. The clerk of the market signaled the opening by ringing the bell that hung in the market house's cupola. Today's Market House is again a commercial and social center with food, toys, and housewares among the goods for sale.

A market house was erected in Williamsburg in the late 1750s. It's unclear how long it stood, though it still appears on a 1781 map. By 1796 the market was housed in the magazine where it remained until a new market house, which did not survive long, was built in the early 1830s.

In 2013 Colonial Williamsburg's archaeologists opened large squares of earth on the site searching for signs of the market house. They did not find the foundations of the building because the site had been compromised by a church built in the mid-1850s. However, they did find brick particles indicating where there had been brick paving defining a broad market square. In addition, they discovered two deep trenches that had been dug during the Revolutionary War without destroying the market building itself. These trenches fixed the area within which the building must have sat, which conformed closely to the size of a building shown on an early map. To determine the fixtures and features of Williamsburg's market, the Foundation's architectural historians studied surviving markets and the records of other cities' markets. Colonial Williamsburg's carpenters and brick masons completed the reconstruction of the building in 2015.

82 Pump House
Open to the public

The Market Square Pump House reflects the common practice of locating public sources of water near marketplaces in the eighteenth century. From Norfolk to Philadelphia, cities intended such pumps to provide a source of drinking water for households without their own wells while also helping the clerk of the market keep the paved marketplace clean. An octagonal pump house was reconstructed in 1950, with the pump design loosely based on one in Harvard Yard in Cambridge, Massachusetts.

83, 84 Magazine and Guardhouse
Magazine open to ticket holders; Guardhouse private

The spark that ignited the Revolution in Virginia was struck at the magazine, which housed weapons and ammunition. On the night of April 20, 1775, British marines, under orders from the governor, Lord Dunmore, broke into the magazine and took fifteen half barrels of powder. The next day, an angry crowd gathered on Market Square, where leaders such as Peyton Randolph called for calm. A little more than a week later, word reached Williamsburg of a similar attempt to seize arms and ammunition in Massachusetts, and at Lexington and Concord fighting broke out. Revolution soon came to Virginia as well; on June 9, Dunmore fled Williamsburg and took refuge on a British ship.

An original building, the magazine was erected in 1715 after Lieutenant Governor Alexander Spotswood requested a "good, substantial House of Brick" to store arms and ammunition. Spotswood himself is credited with the magazine's unusual octagonal design—a design more common for an English garden setting than for a utilitarian structure. A high wall and a guardhouse were added for increased security at the time of the French and Indian War.

After the government moved to Richmond, the magazine became, successively, a market, a Baptist meetinghouse, a Confederate arsenal, a dancing school, and a livery stable. In 1934–1935 Colonial Williamsburg restored the building and reconstructed the perimeter wall and the guardhouse, both of which had been pulled down in the nineteenth century.

At the Magazine today, you can learn about eighteenth-century military activities and view a collection of firearms, both reproductions and antiques.

85 Courthouse
Open to ticket holders

The Courthouse is in the center of town—fittingly so, since what happened here was central to local government. Benjamin Waller, the city's mayor, stood on the courthouse steps on July 25, 1776, to read aloud, for the first time in Williamsburg, the Declaration of Independence.

The building functioned much like a city hall. Government meetings for James City County and the City of Williamsburg took place here, and elections for the House of Burgesses took place just outside the courthouse.

Both civil and criminal cases were held here, though felonies were generally tried at the General Court, which met at the Capitol. All

NATIVE AMERICAN PROGRAMS

Native Americans were a regular presence in Williamsburg during the eighteenth century, and they are again today. Some met with the governor to negotiate treaties they hoped would stop or slow the spread of white settlers. Others came to trade. Then and now, the Native peoples in Williamsburg represent a range of cultures.

In the Historic Area today, visitors can learn about Native histories and cultures and can also see demonstrations of different traditions, including storytelling, dancing, and crafts, from making baskets to making bows.

cases involving enslaved people accused of crimes were tried at the courthouse.

Court days drew crowds of onlookers, and today you can again watch cases in which someone is charged with not attending church, or an apprentice is complaining about a master, or a debtor and a creditor are facing off, or a customer is unhappy with damaged goods, or perhaps someone is charged with stealing a pig. Guests may have the chance to participate as a defendant or witness or justice. Some found guilty might be sentenced to the public stocks, which you can try out for yourself right outside the Courthouse.

Like many Virginia courthouses, this one is T-shaped with a central courtroom, side rooms for juries, and a clerk's office. Built in 1770–1771, its formal design elements—brick walls, round-headed windows, cantilevered pediment, columned portico, wide stair platform, and octagonal cupola (with its original weather vane)—reinforce the building's official appearance.

Unlike other government buildings, the courthouse continued to serve many of the same functions after the capital moved to Richmond. Indeed, the building continued to be used as a courthouse until 1931. The exterior was restored the next year, including the removal of columns that had been added in 1911. In 1991 the colonial courtroom fittings were restored.

Francis Street

86 Ewing House
Private

When Ebenezer Ewing, a Scottish merchant, died in 1795, he left his house to Elizabeth Ashton, the mother of their illegitimate son, Thomas. Elizabeth died four years later, and young Thomas inherited the dwelling. In 1805, the Williamsburg Hustings Court ordered the boy's legal guardian to bond him out for three years to learn the art of seamanship. Thomas disappeared before completing his apprenticeship. The Ewing House and the Ewing Shop behind it are today hotel accommodations.

87 Moody House
Private

Blacksmith Josias Moody owned this one-story frame house from 1794 until he died about 1810. The house, which likely dates from between

1725 and 1750, was altered several times before reaching its present size and appearance by 1782. Though the house survived into the twentieth century, its frame was found to be in such poor condition that it needed to be entirely reconstructed in 1940. The kitchen behind the house is now a hotel facility.

88 Dr. Barraud House
Private

Apothecary William Carter or blacksmith James Anderson likely erected this building as a rental property in the 1760s or early 1770s. Like most buildings in eighteenth-century Williamsburg, the house was altered to suit changing needs and fashion. It reached its present dimensions by 1796. The owner at that time was Dr. Philip Barraud, who had served in the army during the Revolutionary War and later was a visiting physician at the Public Hospital. No major exterior changes were necessary when the house was restored in 1942.

89 Lewis House
Private

Charles Lewis owned the property and is believed to have built the side-passage house that stood here. The house was reconstructed on its eighteenth-century foundations in 1948–1949 and now serves as hotel accommodations.

90 Orrell House
Private

Probably built between 1750 and 1775, this house takes its name from John Orrell, who acquired the property about 1810. The house is proportioned as a geometric cube whose sides each measure twenty-eight feet and whose roof ridge is twenty-eight feet above the top of the basement wall. Restored in 1931, today it is a hotel facility.
91 Orrell Kitchen, behind the house, is the check-in location for guests staying at the Colonial Houses.

92 The Quarter
Private

This early nineteenth-century cottage was named "The Quarter" during the restoration in the 1930s when it was described as having been occupied by a black family around the time of the Civil War. Though clearly a modest building, its prominent location on the street argues against its interpretation as a slave quarter. No purpose-built slave quarters have been identified in Williamsburg. It is now a hotel facility.

Lightfoot Tenement

93 Richard Crump House
Private

Richard Crump owned this house in the eighteenth century. It was reconstructed in 1950 and today is a hotel facility.

94, 95 Bracken Kitchen and Tenement
Private

The one-story Bracken Tenement has a steep gable roof and massive T-shaped exterior chimneys laid in English bond. By the end of the eighteenth century, it was in the possession of the Reverend John Bracken, who had extensive real estate holdings along Francis Street. His rise to social and financial prominence began in 1776 with his marriage to Sally Burwell of Carter's Grove plantation. He was the rector of Bruton Parish Church for forty-five years. In 1815, one observer recounted that the "Round Bellied Vicar" arrived an hour late for a wedding, having imbibed a drop too much en route. This, one of the vicar's rental properties, survived to be restored by the Foundation in 1928. The gardens at the Bracken Tenement feature yaupon holly as an enclosing hedge, as topiary accents, and in a natural screen. Today, the kitchen is a hotel facility.

96, 97 Masonic Lodge and Kitchen
Private

The "ancient and loyal Society of free and accepted Masons" leased a portion of this lot and met in a building on this property from the 1780s onward. In the 1770s, the lodge held its regular meetings at Market Square Tavern. Members of the Williamsburg chapter included Peyton Randolph, Peter Pelham, Bishop James Madison, St. George Tucker, and James Monroe. The lodge was reconstructed in 1931. Today, the kitchen is a hotel facility.

98 Lightfoot House
Private

Built in the mid-1700s probably as a rental property, this house was brought to its final form by 1750 as a town house for the prominent Lightfoot family of Yorktown. The fine brick residence is unusual in having a second floor as high as the first. It is adorned by a string-course in molded brick and by a wrought-iron balcony suggestive of the one at the Governor's Palace. The decorative front fence shows the Chinese, or chinoiserie, influence popular about 1750. During restoration in 1940–1941, the ornate wrought-iron balcony was reconstructed based on evidence in the brickwork. Such a feature would have been a clear sign of the Lightfoot family's prominence since the form is associated with public, not private, buildings in this period.

99 Lightfoot Tenement
Private

The Reverend John Bracken, who bought the Lightfoot House in 1786, also bought this property. Based on its small size, orientation to the street, and surviving foundations, the structure was likely a store. It was reconstructed in 1961. Today, it is a hotel facility.

100, 101 Nicholas-Tyler Office and Nicholas-Tyler Laundry
Private

These two buildings mark the site of the Nicholas-Tyler House. Robert Carter Nicholas, treasurer of the colony of Virginia and later a judge of the Chancery Court, bought the property in 1770 and built a large frame house with numerous outbuildings. John Tyler and his family were living here when two horsemen pulled up in front of the house in 1841 and delivered the news that President William Henry Harrison had died and Tyler was to become the tenth president of the United States. The office and laundry were reconstructed in 1941 and are now hotel accommodations.

Nicholson Street

102 Elizabeth Reynolds House
Private
In 1777, *Virginia Gazette* printer William Hunter deeded a narrow strip of land containing a house and garden to his mother, Elizabeth Reynolds. Hunter was illegitimate, and although his father had acknowledged William in his will, he failed to provide for the boy's mother. The house was reconstructed in 1958.

103 Hay's Cabinetmaking Shop
Open to ticket holders
Cabinetmakers today use eighteenth-century tools and techniques to produce fine furniture where Anthony Hay purchased a shop in 1756 but may have been practicing the trade as early as 1750. Hay ran the shop until late 1766 or early 1767 when he leased it to furniture maker Benjamin Bucktrout and later to Edmund Dickinson, who was killed at the Battle of Monmouth in 1778. Bucktrout advertised that he would also make and repair harpsichords and spinets, and that trade is also carried on at the shop today. The cabinetmakers also do carving; for example, they ornament furniture and frames.

The wareroom through which you enter the shop displays a sampling of the work done here, including a harpsichord and a desk with secret compartments for storing documents and money. The furniture made at the shop appealed to gentry as well as to merchants, who wanted furniture as fashionable as what could be found in London.

Archaeologists found the remains of a fence rail in the streambed under the shop, and this rail was the basis for the design of the fence in front of the shop. The shop spans a little creek, though it wasn't used for waterpower; the stream was too weak to drive a wheel with any force. Rather, the shop was built here because it was near Hay's home, which once stood on the lot to the west, and because, being in a ravine, it was a comparatively undesirable piece of real estate for a residence. The wing that spans the creek was probably added by Hay in the late 1750s. The building was reconstructed in 1965.

Historic Farmer
Open to ticket holders
Historic farmers grow tobacco, corn, and cotton using eighteenth-century techniques and tools. The crops are heirloom varieties not commonly found today. Check at a ticket office for location.

104 Ludwell-Paradise Stable
Private

The stable was reconstructed in 1932 based on precedents found at the Botetourt Hotel in Gloucester County and the tavern stable at the King William County Courthouse, both since torn down.

105, 106, 107 Tayloe House, Office, and Kitchen
Private

This frame house was built between 1752 and 1759. John Tayloe, a prominent planter, bought the house in 1759 to serve as his town residence after he was appointed to the governor's Council. The Dutch, or gambrel, roof has two separate slopes to provide more headroom in the upper story. A distinctive architectural refinement is the elongated kick, or upturn, on the lower eaves. The building is largely original, though the platform of the reconstructed porch is paved with fragments of English Portland stone found on the site during excavation. The most conspicuous of the surviving outbuildings is the office with its ogee, or bell-shaped, roof. The office is largely original. It and the house were restored, and the kitchen reconstructed, in 1951.

AX RANGE

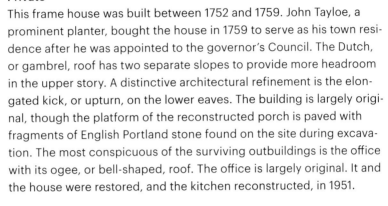

Belt axes were standard-issue in many units of the Revolution, when they were used for clearing brush and cutting wood. They were not generally thrown in combat; instead, ax throwing was a downtime activity for troops. In April 1776, orders were issued to the Fifth Virginia Regiment in Williamsburg "to take care that no injury is done to the Trees ... by the Custom of Throwing Tomahawks."

At the Ax Range, at the corner of Nicholson and Botetourt Streets, guests learn about the history of military axes. After a safety presentation, you can test your skill throwing at targets. Must be age twelve or older to participate. Guests younger than seventeen must be accompanied by an adult eighteen or older. All participants must wear closed-toe shoes.

108 Ludwell Tenement
Private

One characteristic of Williamsburg's backstreets was that rental properties and smaller houses, such as this one, which was reconstructed in 1953, coexisted with the homes of well-to-do neighbors such as the Randolphs and the Tayloes.

109 Brickyard
Open to ticket holders

Bricks are made here as they were in the eighteenth century and, for that matter, much as they were five thousand years ago. What you see at the Brickyard depends on what season you arrive. In the spring and summer, brickmakers use their feet to mix the clay. Then they mold the clay into bricks. In the fall, they stack about twenty thousand bricks to form a kiln and fire it up.

Kids who like to get muddy love to get in the treading pit. But brickmaking was hard work, and in the eighteenth century, children might be tasked with carrying the bricks from where they were molded to beds where they would dry. Men, women, and children, often enslaved, worked at the trade. Often bricks were made at or near building sites, and unlike most other trades, the client often provided materials and labor.

Today bricks made at the Brickyard are used in building and repairing foundations, chimneys, walkways, and buildings throughout the Historic Area. The masonry tradespeople also transform oyster shells into lime to make the mortar to build and repair buildings.

110 Peyton Randolph House
Open to ticket holders

The home of one of Williamsburg's most prominent families, the Peyton Randolph House also provides a look at the lives of the enslaved people who worked in and around the house.

Peyton and Betty Randolph were an eighteenth-century version of a power couple. Peyton Randolph represented the colony as the attorney general while his private practice served clients such as George Washington. He was Speaker of the House of Burgesses from 1766 to 1775 and president of the First Continental Congress. Elizabeth "Betty" Randolph was born into the influential Harrison family. After Peyton died in 1775, Betty remained in Williamsburg and allowed the comte de Rochambeau to use her home as his headquarters while he and Washington planned the siege of Yorktown.

Betty and Peyton had no children, but the larger Randolph family was torn apart by the Revolution. Peyton was a leading patriot; his brother John was a Loyalist who returned to England in the fall of 1775. John's son, Edmund, joined Washington's troops as the general's aide-de-camp and later became attorney general and then secretary of state of the United States.

The Randolphs were free to devote their time to such causes because of the twenty-eight enslaved people who worked in and around the house. These included Peyton Randolph's manservant, John Harris, who accompanied him to Philadelphia and witnessed the proceedings of the Continental Congress. After Peyton's death, Edmund Randolph inherited Harris. Harris must have run away since in December 1777 Edmund Randolph placed an ad in the *Virginia Gazette* offering a reward of five dollars *"to any person who will apprehend Johnny, otherwise called John Harris, a mulatto man slave who formerly waited upon my uncle."*

Another enslaved member of the household, known only as Eve, was probably the personal maid of Betty Randolph. An inventory of Peyton Randolph's estate valued her at one hundred British pounds,

The FATHER of HIS COUNTRY

In 1774, Peyton Randolph was elected the first president of the Continental Congress, leading the British to place him on a list of those they proposed to hang. When Randolph returned to Williamsburg, members of the militia offered to protect him in an address that concluded: "MAY HEAVEN GRANT YOU LONG TO LIVE THE FATHER OF YOUR COUNTRY, AND THE FRIEND TO FREEDOM AND HUMANITY!" It was not until the next year that anyone thought to call George Washington the nation's father. Had Randolph not died in October 1775, leading to John Hancock's election as president of the Continental Congress, it might very well have been Randolph's and not Hancock's signature above all others on the Declaration of Independence.

suggesting she was highly skilled. In 1780, when British forces occupied Williamsburg, Eve sought freedom behind their lines with her fourteen-year-old son, George. Eve was later recaptured, and Betty Randolph sold her because of what she called her "bad behaviour."

The western portion of the house, on the corner of Nicholson and North England Streets, was built in 1715–1718 by William Robertson, clerk of the governor's Council. Peyton's father, Sir John Randolph, was living here in 1724 when he bought the lot and the one-story house next door. Sir John was the only Virginian knighted by the Crown. In 1754–1755, Peyton Randolph linked the two buildings with the two-story central section featuring a grand stairway lighted by a monumental roundheaded window and an elegant dining room with a bedchamber above. Peyton and Betty Randolph had the old kitchen torn down and replaced with a much larger one that contained laundry facilities, slave quarters, and a cellar with a covered way connecting it to the main house. The roof is hipped on the west and gabled on the east, reflecting the two periods of construction.

Colonial Williamsburg restored the building in 1939–1940 and again in 1967–1968. Original paneling survives in several rooms as well as a marble mantle in the dining room. In 1997, Colonial Williamsburg tradespeople used eighteenth-century materials, tools, and techniques to reconstruct the kitchen, the passageway connecting it to the main house, a smokehouse, a milk house, and other service buildings.

PATRIOTS *at* PLAY

Colonial days were not all work, and in the Randolph yard you can sample a range of fun activities for families. You might play draughts (sort of like checkers) or ninepins (like bowling) or loggets (like horseshoes), which King Henry VIII banned because he worried it would distract his soldiers from their duties. Or you might try your hand at making marbles from clay or building a willow wattle fence. There are also opportunities to learn about rare breeds—animals that were a big part of life in Williamsburg during the eighteenth century and again today. Open seasonally.

111 Grissell Hay Lodging House
Private

The core of this house, conceivably one of the first houses on Market Square, may date as early as 1717, when it belonged to Dr. Archibald Blair. Apothecary Peter Hay lived here in the 1760s. After Hay's death, his widow, Grissell, operated a lodging house here. During the house's 1930–1931 restoration, nineteenth-century windows were replaced with sash windows of an eighteenth-century type. The architects chose to retain the early nineteenth-century front porch with its Doric columns and pediment, though it postdates the colonial period, because it illustrates the continued use of the classical architectural tradition. The kitchen, dairy, smokehouse, and privy, which date from the early nineteenth century, are among the few surviving early outbuildings in the Historic Area.

112 St. George Tucker House
Open to select donor society members

St. George Tucker, who was a professor of law at the College of William & Mary, bought this property in 1788. He moved an older building, a one-story dwelling built nearby in 1716–1717 by William Levingston, to this site, reoriented the house toward Market Square, placed it on new raised brick foundations, and enlarged it. Over the next six years, Tucker added a second story, a flanking one-story wing, and a kitchen. Accounts for all this work survive, making the construction of this building the best documented in Williamsburg. The house was renovated in 1930–1931 but not fully restored to its eighteenth-century appearance. Many of the Greek Revival details of nineteenth-century renovations were changed to imitate colonial ones, but the form of the building was not changed. The kitchen at the west end of the complex was reconstructed. Today, the house is Colonial Williamsburg's donor reception center.

On path to Visitor Center

113 Great Hopes Plantation
Open to ticket holders

Most colonial Virginians, free and enslaved, did not live on large plantations or in towns like Williamsburg. Great Hopes represents the many middling plantations that existed near the capital. Today you can tour the site on your own.

114 Windmill
Private

Windmills were a common sight in colonial Virginia. In the early 1720s, lawyer William Robertson operated a mill in the vicinity of the Peyton Randolph House. The 1782 Frenchman's Map also shows a post windmill located south of the Public Hospital. The Windmill at Great Hopes, completed in 1957, stood for fifty-three years behind the Peyton Randolph House. Since a windmill and the current configuration of the Peyton Randolph House never coexisted, and the likely historic location of the windmill was farther to the north, the structure was moved to its current location in 2010. Based on the 1636 Bourn Mill in Cambridgeshire, England, this form, called a *post-mill,* has the superstructure revolving on top of a single timber post. The upper floor holds the main wind shaft and millstones; the lower floor holds the bolting, or sifting, apparatus. Windmills required constant attention to ensure that they faced the wind and that the grinding and bolting operations ran properly. For post-mills, if the wind changed direction, the miller lifted the stairs and pushed on the tail pole and wheel to turn the mill to face the wind. This reconstructed post-mill is one of the most accurate representations of an eighteenth-century mill in the United States.

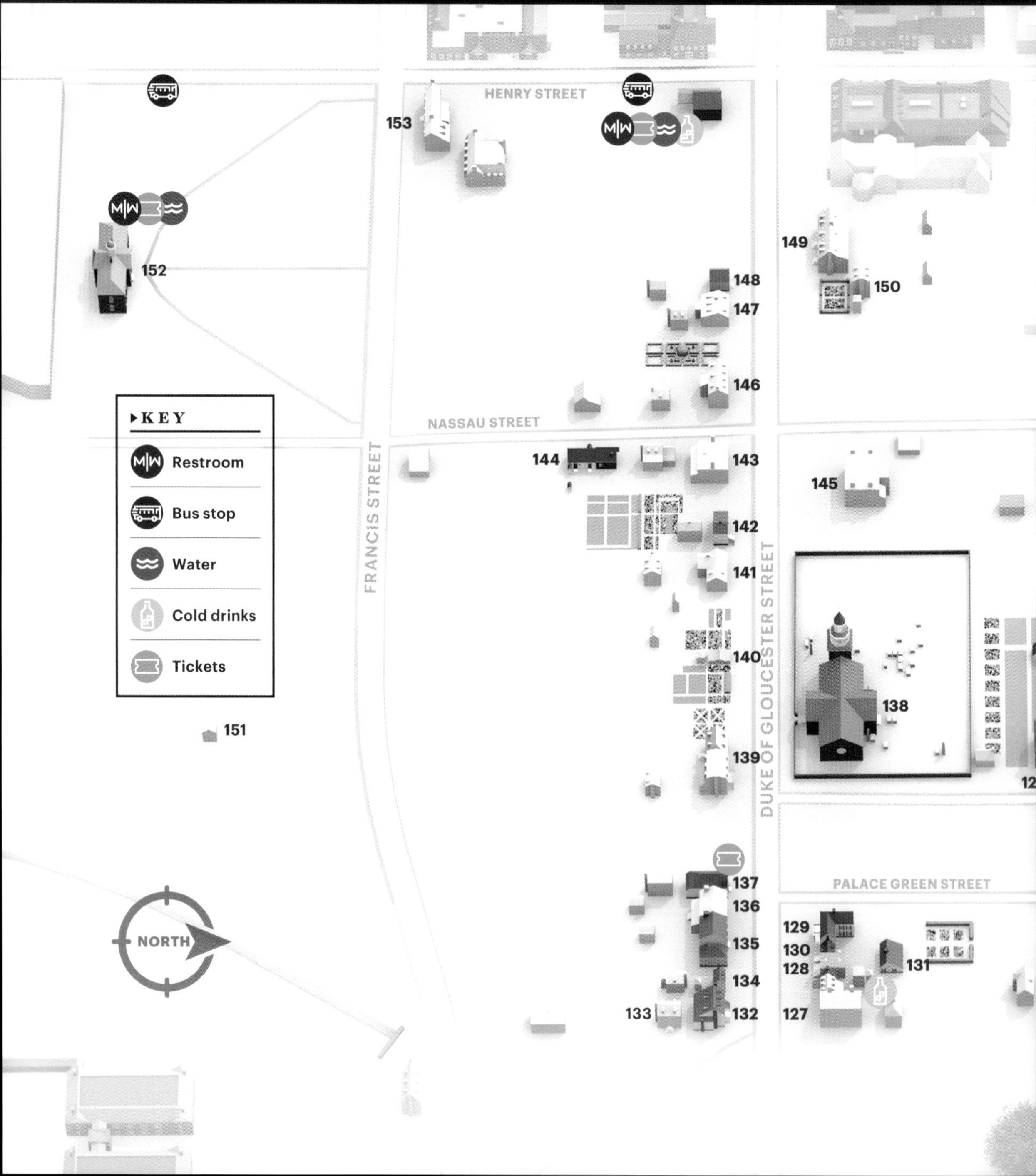

HENRY STREET

153

152

▶ KEY

M|W	Restroom
🚌	Bus stop
≈	Water
🍾	Cold drinks
🎫	Tickets

151

NORTH

NASSAU STREET

FRANCIS STREET

148
147

146

144
143

145

142

141

140

138

139

DUKE OF GLOUCESTER STREET

149
150

137
136

135

134

133 132

PALACE GREEN STREET

129
130
128
127

131

NASSAU STREET

PRINCE GEORGE STREET

121

123

120

119

117

118

116

115

PALACE GREEN STREET

126

125

124

SCOTLAND STREET

LAFAYETTE STREET

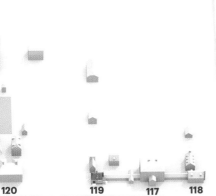

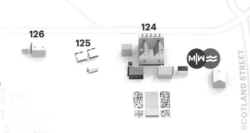

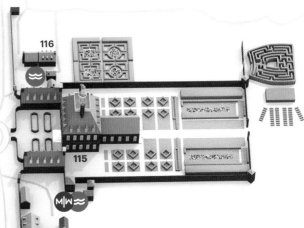

Palace Green

115 Governor's Palace
Open to ticket holders

As a symbol of British imperial authority in colonial Virginia, the Governor's Palace was one of the finest residences in British America, prominently sited at the end of a broad green. The visibility, scale, and formality of the house and its two advance buildings reinforced the power of the royal governor. So too did the gates, with their heraldic lion and unicorn and a crown, as well as the imposing display of arms in the entry and the elegant furnishings throughout the house.

No provision was made for an official residence in the 1699 plan for the town, but after several years of housing the colony's executive in rented properties, construction began on the Palace in 1706, during the administration of Governor Edward Nott. The house was not completed until 1722. Much of the construction and decoration was overseen by Governor Alexander Spotswood, whose vision brought forth the elaborate gardens and the impressive arms display but also led to serious cost overruns. Virginians complained that their governor "lavishes away the Country's money," but visitors to Williamsburg praised him for creating one of the greatest structures in British America. Rich and powerful planters in the colony followed his lead and built great plantation houses of their own, such as Rosewell in Gloucester County, Stratford Hall in Westmoreland, and Shirley in nearby Charles City County.

The servants—both paid and enslaved—who worked at the Palace came from a variety of backgrounds and practiced many trades required to maintain the prestige of the house. The kitchen, scullery, laundry, and other support buildings needed to maintain the household are located in the west yard. The kitchen was one of the finest in Virginia, and today Historic Foodways staff demonstrate the high style of cooking there.

Later governors continued to improve and enlarge the official residence. The ballroom and supper room wing was added as part of a refurbishment undertaken for the arrival of Lieutenant Governor Robert Dinwiddie in 1751. The seventh and final royal governor, John Murray, the Earl of Dunmore, arrived in 1771 amid growing discontent with the old social, political, and cultural order. Dunmore's efforts to uphold royal authority only fueled Virginians' desire for independence. After the governor ordered gunpowder seized from the magazine and threatened to arm slaves against rebellious colonists, he was forced to flee the Palace under cover of darkness. A year after Dunmore and his family left, the independent Commonwealth of Virginia auctioned off the family's belongings, including enslaved servants.

The first two governors of the Commonwealth of Virginia, Patrick Henry and Thomas Jefferson, also lived at the Palace. During his residence, Governor Henry not only oversaw Virginia's participation in the Revolutionary War but also found time to marry Dorothea Dandridge, the granddaughter of Governor Spotswood.

Jefferson lived here with his wife, Martha; their daughters; and the Hemings family of enslaved men and women. While living in the Palace, he sketched a series of drawings as part of his plan to remodel the building a second time. These expansive plans were never carried out since the capital (and the governor) moved from Williamsburg to Richmond in 1780.

Following the siege of Yorktown, American forces used the Palace as a hospital. In December 1781, fire destroyed the building.

Archaeological excavation of the Palace complex began in 1930, and the reconstruction was completed in 1934. That work was greatly aided by Jefferson's drawings, which included room dimensions, ceiling heights, wall thicknesses, window placements, and chimneys. Also key to the reconstruction was a copper plate engraving discovered in England's Bodleian Library in 1929, which showed the Palace and its two advance buildings as seen from Palace Green.

The Bodleian Plate was also helpful in re-creating the Palace's elaborate complex of gardens. Features include the original eighteenth-century falling gardens (terraces) and canal.

116 Foodways (Governor's Palace Kitchen)
Open to ticket holders

In the Historic Area you can not only experience the sights and sounds of eighteenth-century Virginia but also the smells. Members of Colonial Williamsburg's Foodways team re-create dishes from plum pudding to flip (a beverage of eggs, cream, beer, and spices) in the Governor's Palace kitchen. Special programs include demonstrations of brewing and chocolate making.

Then as now, food did more than fill stomachs. The cooks at the Palace prepared French-influenced cuisine that reinforced the governor's social position. Enslaved cooks at kitchens throughout the town blended techniques and tastes from Europe and Africa to create a uniquely Virginian cuisine. A poor household, by contrast, often had just one pot, in which to make soups and porridges.

SPEAKING TERMS

Rare Breeds

>

The Rare Breeds program presents animals that were or could have been here in the eighteenth century and might not be here if not for preservation efforts. Please don't feed or pet them.

- **Leicester Longwool Sheep—** A sheep known for its long, lustrous wool that falls in ringlets. George Washington raised Leicester Longwools at Mount Vernon, and his step-grandson used them to develop the first American breed of sheep.

- **American Cream Draft Horses—** A horse characterized by its medium cream-colored coat, pink skin, amber eyes, long white mane and tail, and white markings. The only modern breed in the program is also the rarest— just over five hundred exist in North America.

- **Cleveland Bay Horses—**A rich reddish-brown colored horse with black legs, mane, and tail.

- **American Milking Devon Cattle—**A breed producing milk that contains a high butterfat content, prized in the eighteenth century for butter and cheese. They also provide quality meat and are good work animals.

- **Milking Shorthorn Oxen—**Red or white cattle trained to work. These oxen served as the trucks and tractors of the eighteenth century.

- **Dominique Chickens—**A small to medium chicken with a hardy constitution and heavy plumage. It was one of the first breeds developed in America.

- **Nankin Bantam Chickens—** A golden bird with red combs and shiny black feathers. It was known as a yellow bantam in colonial times. The hens are broody, meaning they like to sit on anything and were therefore used to hatch pheasant and quail eggs.

Robert Carter House

Health and safety regulations preclude guests from sampling the fare, but you can find some recipes at recipes.history.org.

117, 118 Robert Carter House and Office
Private

Long thought to have been constructed in the late 1740s, the Robert Carter House was actually built in 1727. The new date, the result of dendrochronological (tree-ring) testing, reveals that the house was built while the property was owned by Robert "King" Carter. Carter's nickname came about because he was the richest man in Virginia with over three hundred thousand acres of land. He was also one of the most powerful—serving as Speaker of the House of Burgesses, as a member of the governor's Council, and in 1726–1727, while the house was being built, as acting governor.

The house is unusual for Williamsburg in that it is oriented both toward Palace Green in front and toward gardens in the rear, much as a James River plantation house of this period faced both road and river. Instead of outbuildings and work yards behind the house, the Carter House looked out over a series of man-made earthen terraces that are still visible today. The service buildings that are found directly behind the main house on most Williamsburg properties are here sited to the sides, permitting elegant vistas from the rear rooms instead of a view of work in the kitchen and laundry.

Robert Carter III, King Carter's grandson, lived in the house from 1761 to 1772 and owned the house until 1801. He made significant improvements during his occupation, updating the trim in some rooms and installing fashionable wallpaper throughout the house. He used the largest and best finished room on the ground floor, facing the rear gardens, as his dining room. The large front room, facing Palace Green, was his study, which contained not only an impressive library of books on religion, philosophy, and the law but also a chamber organ and other musical instruments. Over the Revolutionary years, Robert Carter III's antislavery feelings grew to the point that he made the extraordinary decision to free his entire enslaved workforce of over five hundred people from his eighteen landholdings.

Restored in 1931–1932 and 1951–1953, the house and brick kitchen are original. Other structures, including the office and the covered way, are reconstructions.

119 McKenzie Shop
Open to the public

Dr. Kenneth McKenzie owned and lived on this property from 1747 to 1751. He likely built his apothecary shop soon after moving to the site. Among other bequests, he left to his friend Dr. James Carter a skeleton. Colonial Williamsburg rebuilt the shop in 1952. Today the shop is a small counter-service concession offering drinks and light refreshments that is open seasonally.

120 Elkanah Deane House
Private

This house was named for an Irish coachmaker who paid seven hundred pounds in 1772 for four lots and the original dwelling, shop, and garden on this site. Elkanah Deane may have been encouraged to move to Williamsburg from New York by Royal Governor Lord Dunmore, for whom he had made a coach, phaeton, and riding chair.

The original house was likely built soon after 1720 when the property was sold to John Holloway. Before its purchase by Elkanah Deane, it was also the home of Dr. John de Sequeyra, eighteenth-century Williamsburg's only known resident of Jewish descent. De Sequeyra treated many Williamsburg residents during the smallpox epidemic of 1747–1748 and was one of the first attending physicians at the Public Hospital. The Deane House was reconstructed in 1939.

121 Wheelwright (Elkanah Deane Shop)
Open to ticket holders

Just off Palace Green, behind the Elkanah Deane House, is the Elkanah Deane Shop. Deane probably built a shop soon after his purchase in 1772 because he knew that his carriage-making business would cater to wealthy clients like those who lived near the Governor's Palace.

In the late eighteenth century, wheelwrights, blacksmiths, and harness makers all worked on the site to make carts, wheelbarrows, wagons, riding chairs, and carriages. Today, wheelwrights at the shop make hubs, spokes, and rims from wood. An iron tire usually circles the rim's exterior. The wheels were built to last, even on rough colonial roads. Today's wheelwrights also build and repair entire vehicles at the site. The building was reconstructed in 1936.

122 George Wythe House
Open to ticket holders

Enter the George Wythe House and you are entering the world of the Enlightenment. Like other Enlightenment thinkers, Wythe believed that there was nothing in the natural world men could not understand and that citizens had the right—indeed, the obligation—to explore that world. In this house, Wythe's students—among them Thomas Jefferson—contemplated law and philosophy and science . . . and the ideas that propelled the American Revolution. John Adams believed that he and Wythe and their contemporaries had "been sent into life, at a time when the greatest law-givers of antiquity would have wished to have lived."

Wythe lived here from about 1755, around the time he married Elizabeth Taliaferro, until 1791. The house is among Williamsburg's most elegant. Built in the mid-1750s, it is believed to have been designed by Wythe's father-in-law Richard Taliaferro, and its masonry is some of the best work in town—its rubbed-and-gauged jack arches are especially well-made. Impressive as its mass is, with its great chimneys rising through a high hipped roof, the real achievement of its design is its subtlety. The second-story windows, for example, are slightly smaller than those on the first, but this difference is concealed by using the same number of windowpanes for windows on both levels. Similarly, the space between the windows and the corner of the house is identical on the front and sides.

On the interior, the striking Prussian blue wallpaper is based on architectural and documentary evidence (and is similar to contemporary paper used in Britain's Windsor Castle). The house is furnished with items that reveal Wythe's wide-ranging interests. In Wythe's

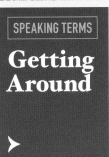

Getting Around

- **Carriage**—Any two- or four-wheeled vehicle used to convey people.

- **Cart**—A two-wheeled vehicle used primarily to haul freight.

- **Chaise**—A two-wheeled vehicle like a riding chair but with a top.

- **Coach**—A four-wheeled enclosed vehicle with two seats facing each other. A coach can hold four to six passengers.

- **Landau**—A form of coach with a two-piece leather top that can be separated and folded down.

- **Riding Chair**—A two-wheeled vehicle for one or two people. These are light, airy, easy to maneuver, and relatively expensive and were quite common in Williamsburg in the eighteenth century, especially among the upper and middle classes.

- **Sociable**—An open carriage with two seats facing each other. Often called a *phaeton*.

- **Stage Wagon**—A vehicle developed for public transportation.

- **Oxcart**—A general purpose cart not generally used for carrying passengers—except for the most adventurous!

Colonial Williamsburg offers carriage and wagon rides and special interest tours of the stables featuring carriages and horses. For details, see colonialwilliamsburg.org.

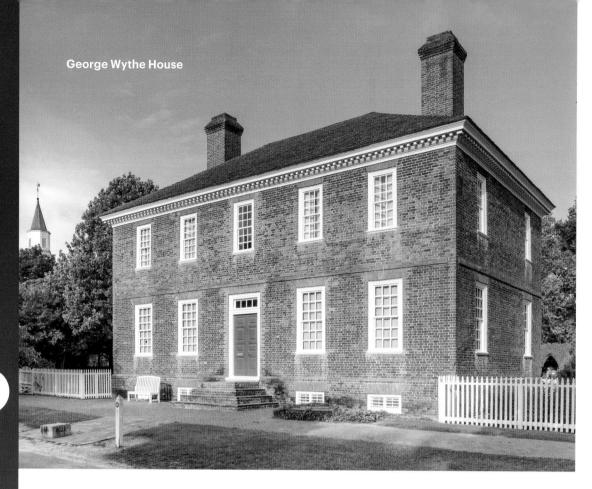

George Wythe House

PROFESSOR WYTHE

George Wythe was a member of the House of Burgesses, a delegate to the Continental Congress and the Constitutional Convention, and a signer of the Declaration of Independence. Yet perhaps his most profound legacy was as a teacher. His students included Thomas Jefferson, future chief justice of the United States John Marshall, and future secretary of state and Speaker of the House Henry Clay.

Wythe became America's first law professor in 1779 when the College of William & Mary appointed him professor of law and police. Prior to Wythe's appointment, legal education came not in schools but as apprenticeships. Jefferson served as Wythe's legal apprentice between 1762 and 1765. In 1821, at the age of seventy-seven and looking back on his youth, Jefferson described Wythe as "my faithful and beloved Mentor in youth, and my most affectionate friend through life."

Marshall was a diligent student of Wythe's, though his decision to attend William & Mary may have been motivated in part by Williamsburg's proximity to Yorktown, home of his future wife, Polly Ambler. His notebooks from his college days hint that his mind may have occasionally strayed from Wythe's lectures. Throughout Marshall's notebooks can be found in his handwriting the name "Polly."

office, for example, is a sampling of books; Wythe owned 649 volumes, which he ultimately left to Jefferson. In the dining room is an orrery, a model of the solar system showing the planets, six of which were then known. Upstairs, in the "lumber" room, are fossils, a globe, and a shark tooth—all of which today's students are free to touch. Also available to be touched and read is a copy of the Declaration of Independence, of which Wythe was one of the signers. Note that Wythe's signature appears above those of his fellow Virginians, including Thomas Jefferson, the principal author of the Declaration.

Prior to the siege of Yorktown in 1781, George Washington used Wythe's house as his headquarters. Here Washington met with American and French commanders, including the marquis de Lafayette, to plan for the decisive battle. The enslaved people in the Wythe household, such as his cook Lydia Broadnax, must have noted the contradictions of the Founders' rhetoric: Independence from England would not bring freedom from slavery. Unlike most of his fellow slaveholders, however, Wythe at various times advocated abolition, and later in his life he divested himself of all his slaves, giving some to relatives and freeing others. Among those freed was Broadnax, who continued to work for Wythe.

In the pleasure garden between the kitchen garden and work yard, a pleached American hornbeam arbor serves as the terminal focal point. In addition to a kitchen, there are a variety of dependencies, including stables, a dovecote for housing squabs, a chicken coop, and "necessaries." The laundry is furnished for an enslaved woman, reflecting the common use of outbuildings, especially kitchens and laundries, for housing Williamsburg's slaves.

Behind the garden is a pasture where you can often see various livestock.

All the brickwork in the house is original, except for the chimneys, which had to be rebuilt during the 1939–1940 restoration. The outbuildings are all reconstructed.

123 Cooperage (George Wythe Lumber House)
Open to ticket holders
In the eighteenth century, coopers made the casks in which a vast assortment of goods was shipped—hats, shoes, nails, sugar, salt, rice, leeches, rum, wine, tobacco, and more. In an age without machinery to do the lifting and moving, packaging that rolled was ideal for shipping almost everything.

Coopers made containers of all sizes out of narrow strips of wood called *staves* that were held together by metal or wooden hoops, not by any adhesive. The wood used for the staves included a variety of native timbers such as white and red oaks, chestnut, white cedar, and yellow pine; the key was to choose wood that was straight-grained, free of knots, and split from the log so that it could be shaped quickly and efficiently.

"White" coopers produced straight tapered containers such as buckets, tubs, and churns. "Slack" coopers manufactured casks for the shipment of bulk goods. "Tight" coopers, the most skilled, manufactured containers that could hold liquids without leaking.

Coopers generally specialized in a particular type of cask and worked for that particular business. Coopers who made tobacco containers, for example, worked on plantations where tobacco was produced or at tobacco warehouses. Coopers who made flour casks worked at mills where flour was ground. Most coopers in Williamsburg would have made household items such as buckets and tubs. The casks made at the cooperage behind the George Wythe House are used in other trades shops and exhibition sites throughout the Historic Area.

The only cooperage in Williamsburg about which specific information is known was owned by Adam Waterford, a free African American.

124 Thomas Everard House
Open to ticket holders
The Thomas Everard House is noted for its fine staircase with its turned balusters and richly carved stair brackets. Its rooms have been

SPEAKING TERMS

Tierces and Firkins

›

The sizes of casks and the commodities they would hold were specified by legislation.

Wine (in gallons)	Ale (in gallons)	Beer (in gallons)
Rundlet —18	Firkin — 8	Firkin — 9
Barrel — 31½	Kilderkin — 16	Kilderkin — 18
Tierce — 42	Barrel — 32	Barrel — 36
Hogshead — 63	Hogshead — 48	Hogshead — 54
Puncheon — 84		
Pipe — 126		
Tun — 252		

carefully furnished with antiques that reflect the Virginia-made furniture as well as goods imported from other parts of the British empire that filled the house when Everard lived in it. Everard, who arrived in Virginia as an orphan apprentice in the 1730s, twice served as mayor of Williamsburg. He acquired the property about 1755 and lived here for twenty-five years.

The house was built in 1718 by John Brush, a gunsmith and armorer and first keeper of the public magazine. His three-room house included a hall, parlor, and bedchamber on the ground floor and was one of the first in Williamsburg to have a center passage. After Brush died in 1726, the house had several different owners. After Thomas Everard acquired the property, he improved the woodwork in the principal rooms and added the south wing in the early 1770s to give the house its U-shaped plan.

The house was restored in 1949–1951. The work yard between the house and the outbuildings is paved with the original bricks discovered during archaeological excavations. The wooden smokehouse and the brick kitchen are original buildings that have been restored. The kitchen began as a frame structure on brick foundations with only the chimney end being brick. In 1774, the building was extended to the north, the wooden portions were rebuilt in brick, and dormers were added, probably to ventilate sleeping areas for slaves in the loft.

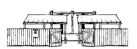

125 Play House Stage
Open to ticket holders
This open-air theater is located on the site of the first theater built in the American colonies, which was active in the 1720s and 1730s. Today, weather permitting, an ensemble presents family-friendly pieces, including plays and music from the period as well as original pieces created in the spirit of the eighteenth century.

Archaeologists unearthed on the site fragmentary foundations likely related to a playhouse built by William Levingston early in the eighteenth century. The two-story wooden structure may have measured as much as eighty-six feet in length by about thirty feet in width, the general size of many English provincial theaters of the period.

126 Levingston Kitchen
Private
Soon after buying three lots at this location in 1716, William Levingston built a house, a kitchen, and other buildings. He also constructed a theater and laid out a bowling green. To date, only the kitchen has been reconstructed, in 1932.

Duke of Gloucester Street

127 Roscow Cole House
Private

Built on the foundations of an earlier colonial frame structure, the main, brick part of the Roscow Cole House was completed between 1809 and 1812. A smaller separate wooden structure was built by 1753 when it was leased to wigmaker John Bryan. That building, with a doorway onto Duke of Gloucester Street, survived into the early nineteenth century. When the main house was restored in 1939, the smaller structure was reconstructed as part of the house.

128 Mary Dickinson Store
Private

Mary Dickinson advertised millinery, jewelry, and other goods for sale *"next Door to Mr.* JAMES GEDDY'S *Shop, near the Church"* in an October 1771 issue of the *Virginia Gazette.* The structure was built about 1755 and restored in 1930.

129, 130 James Geddy House and Shop
Open to ticket holders

The James Geddy House offers a chance to see what family life was like in the eighteenth century. Kids can try on clothes, participate in chores such as sewing and setting the table, and play games like ninepins and quoits.

James Geddy Sr. was not as wealthy as most of his neighbors on Palace Green, but he was a successful gunsmith, and his sons practiced other trades on the property. In the eighteenth century, several busy forges in the foundry behind the house resulted in a yard littered with piles of coal, mounds of slag, and assorted iron and brass waste.

In 1760, his widow, Anne Geddy, sold the property to their son James Jr., who set up shop as a silversmith, goldsmith, and watch repairer. Apparently some customers may have found the location too far from the more commercial neighborhood near the Capitol since in 1772 James Jr. advertised that his prices were so reasonable that they would "remove that Objection of his Shop's being too high up Town."

The house, which was built in 1761–1762 by James Jr., reflected the family's rising social standing. The L-shaped plan was uncommon for Williamsburg and may have been adapted to fit the corner lot. The wing along Palace Green contains the dining room, the largest space in the house, reflecting the importance of dining across a wide range

CAESAR HOPE'S SHOP

John Hope, who was known as Barber Caesar, was enslaved for thirty years before he was granted his freedom in 1779. The *Virginia Gazette* hailed him as "the famous barber of York." Once freed, Hope established himself as an independent businessman and gradually earned the money to purchase his wife, son, and then daughter out of slavery. Hope is the only historical figure portrayed in the Historic Area who was born in Africa, and his story offers a unique perspective on freedom and slavery during America's colonial and Revolutionary eras. Hope's story is interpreted in the rear of the Roscow Cole House in the section that faces Duke of Gloucester Street.

of Williamsburg households in the decades after 1750. It was not just Peyton Randolph and Robert Carter who sought to entertain at home.

The house changed little over the years and was restored in 1930 and again in 1967. It retains much of its eighteenth-century woodwork. Evidence for the reconstructed porch was taken from an outline on the exterior weatherboarding. The one-story retail shop extension to the east was rebuilt on its original foundations.

131 Geddy Foundry
Open to ticket holders

William and David Geddy ran the small brass foundry behind their brother James's house. There they made wares of various metals by melting and pouring them into molds of sand or bronze.

Sand molds could withstand the high heats of the cast iron, sterling, brass, and bronze, but they could only be used once. Pewter, a popular tin alloy that melts around six hundred degrees, could be poured into reusable molds of bronze.

Today founders cast and finish spoons, candlesticks, parts for the silversmiths, carriage and furniture hardware, and many other objects.

132 Weaver (Greenhow Tenement)
Open to ticket holders

Colonists relied heavily on imported fabrics, so when trade with England was restricted during the Revolution, Virginians turned to

A SECRET ADMIRER

One of James Jr. and Elizabeth Geddy's children, Anne (who was known as Nancy), appeared in the "Poets Corner" section of the December 22, 1768, *Virginia Gazette*. An anonymous poet titled his work "*On Miss* ANNE GEDDY *singing, and playing on the* SPINET."

> WHEN Nancy on the spinet plays
> I fondly on the virgin gaze,
> And wish that she was mine;
> Her air, her voice, her lovely face,
> Unite, with such excessive grace,
> The nymph appears divine!

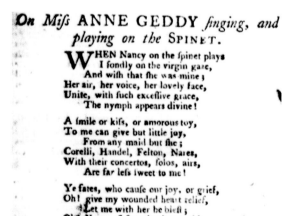

On Miss ANNE GEDDY *singing, and playing on the* SPINET.

WHEN Nancy on the spinet plays
    I fondly on the virgin gaze,
    And wish that she was mine;
Her air, her voice, her lovely face,
Unite, with such exceslive grace,
    The nymph appears divine!

A smile or kifs, or amorous toy,
To me can give but little joy,
    From any maid but she;
Corelli, Handel, Felton, Nares,
With their concertos, folios, airs,
    Are far lefs fweet to me!

Ye fates, who caufe our joy, or grief,
Oh! give my wounded heart relief,
    Let me with her be bleft;
Oh! Venus, foften the dear maid,
Oh! Cupid, grant thy powerful aid,
    And pierce her youthful breaft.

local cloth producers for their textile needs. Small operations continued on plantations, and the Williamsburg Manufactory, which opened in 1776, supplied linen and hempen fabric for the construction of wartime materials—canvas, tents, bedding, and sailcloth.

Today, Colonial Williamsburg weavers spin yarn from raw materials like wool, flax, and cotton. From these spun fibers, they weave cloth on period looms for use throughout the Historic Area. Delving into eighteenth-century dyers' recipe books, they also produce an array of colored fibers and cloth.

The Greenhow Tenement, in which the weavers practice their trade, grew over time. Merchant John Greenhow, who had a large house and store a few doors to the west, owned the building from sometime before 1782 until about 1800. Reconstruction in 1938 was aided by a late nineteenth-century watercolor of the property and by a photograph taken shortly before the building was demolished in the twentieth century.

133 Greenhow Brick Office
Private
Behind the Greenhow Tenement, facing the Magazine, this modest brick structure was once the property of merchant John Greenhow. It may have been built as a combined store and dwelling around 1760. It was restored in 1948.

134 Shoemaker's Shop
Open to ticket holders
In 1773, George Wilson advertised in the *Virginia Gazette* that he specialized in shoes and boots for gentlemen. He also encouraged two or three journeymen shoemakers to apply to him "next Door to Mr. *Greenhow*'s Store." Wilson's was one of about twelve shoemaking operations active in Williamsburg during the 1770s. Assembling a pair of shoes was a day's work for a competent tradesperson.

Shoe shops typically stocked ready-made shoes. Partially due to economy, the fashion of the day called for using straight wooden lasts to shape shoes. Typically, after purchasing a pair of straight shoes, the customer would obtain a right and left fit through wear.

Today, the shoemakers specialize in men's shoes, demonstrating the process while making shoes for Colonial Williamsburg's interpreters and tradespeople.

The tiny shop is typical of a small workplace of the period, with a large window in front to provide light for working through much of the day. Built sometime before 1773, it was restored in 1938.

135, 136 John Greenhow Store and House
Store open to the public; house private

This building, which combines store and house, has three segments. Viewed from the street, from left to right, there are a sloped-roof counting room or office, the entrance to the store, and the doorway to the house. John Greenhow was a merchant in Williamsburg from about 1755 until his death in 1787. The store is the most completely reconstructed eighteenth-century commercial space in Williamsburg. Today it offers some of the same kinds of items Greenhow and his sons sold. Built in the 1750s, the structure was reconstructed in 1953.

137 John Greenhow Lumber House
Open to the public

Greenhow used his lumber house as a stockroom for furniture, barrels, and odds and ends too bulky to keep in his store. In the eighteenth century, *lumber* referred to any sorts of items in storage, rather than construction materials. Today, the building serves as a ticket office. It was reconstructed in 1953.

138 Bruton Parish Church
Open to the public

Thomas Jefferson, George Washington, Patrick Henry, George Wythe, George Mason, and their families worshipped here, as did many other residents of Williamsburg, including enslaved people. It was also the primary place of worship for people from across the colony during Publick Times. The Church of England, which became the Episcopal Church after the Revolution, was state-supported, and free Virginians were required by law to attend services at least once a month. After independence, some members of the church, such as Jefferson, joined with dissenters in a movement to separate church and state. African Americans also worshipped at Bruton Parish, though during the Revolution many formed a church of their own.

The church was the first important public building in Williamsburg, as indicated by its location at the center of the western square of Williamsburg's original plan of 1699. The first brick church was built in 1683. The present structure was completed in 1715. Its cruciform shape arose less from religious symbolism than from a desire to have separate seating sections for different parishioners, with the north and south wings reserved for the governor, members of the Council and House of Burgesses, and provincial officials.

The Reverend W. A. R. Goodwin, who became rector in 1903, spearheaded an early effort to restore the church to its colonial appearance. The interior had been altered several times during the nineteenth century. Goodwin later played a key role in persuading John D. Rockefeller Jr. to fund the restoration of the entire town. A more complete restoration took place in 1938–1939.

The church continues to serve an active congregation, part of the Episcopal diocese of Richmond, but guests are welcome to visit.

139 Custis Tenement
Private

John Custis acquired this lot in 1714 along with two lots to the west. By 1717, he built structures on all three lots and rented them. His son Daniel Parke Custis inherited the property, and when Daniel died, his widow, Martha Custis, administered it. The widow Custis later married George Washington. John Custis was a wealthy, serious-minded gardener whose exchange of plant specimens with English natural historian Peter Collinson aided the restoration of Williamsburg's landscapes. The parterre garden on the west side of the Custis Tenement features formal paths of crushed shell and brick partially enclosed by English boxwood. The house was reconstructed in 1932.

140 Colonial Garden and Nursery
Open to ticket holders

Organic gardening is not a new invention. Back in the eighteenth century, it was the only option, and the historic gardeners at the Colonial Garden use eighteenth-century tools and techniques to grow a wide range of period plants. Guests can learn about eighteenth-century solutions to gardening problems and learn to use tools such as bell jars, hotbeds, and cold frames.

The garden represents a gentleman's pleasure garden. A pleasure garden not only provided food for the table but also flowers, herbs, and plants from around the world. A gentleman's wealth allowed him the leisure time to pursue a passion for gardening and participate in a worldwide plant exchange.

141 Hartwell Perry's Tavern
Private

Hartwell Perry owned and operated an "ordinary," as colonial taverns were sometimes called, on this site from the mid-1780s until he died about 1800. The sign hanging out front is a rebus. It depicts a deer, a well, and several pears. *Hart* is another name for a deer, and an alcoholic beverage made from pears is called a *perry*. The building was reconstructed in 1953.

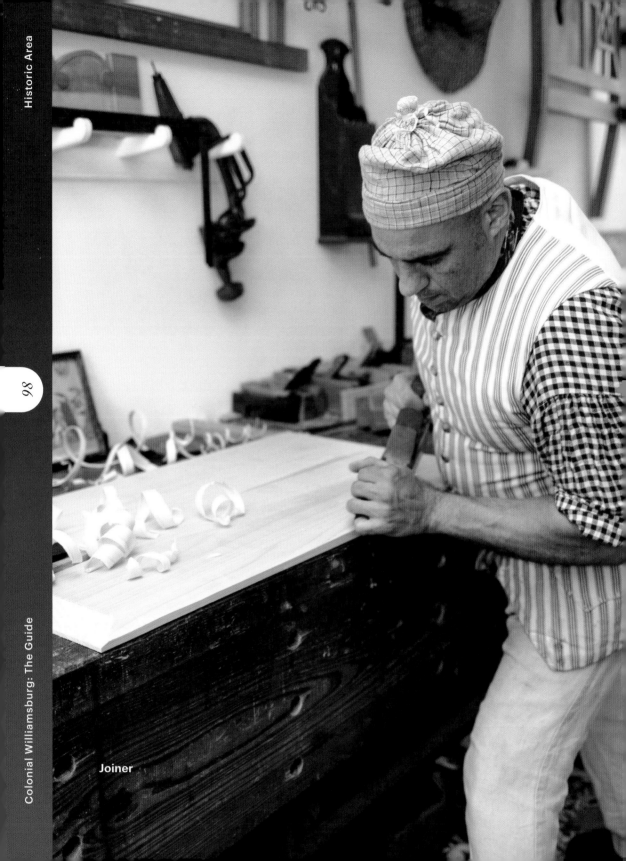

Joiner

142 Joiner (Taliaferro-Cole Shop)
Open to ticket holders

No gentry house in the Historic Area was complete without wooden mantelpieces, moldings, and wainscoting. These elements, along with many other architectural ornaments, were the joiner's responsibility. As woodworkers, joiners can build anything from the most exquisite window sash to the humblest tavern table.

Coachmaker Charles Taliaferro purchased this property, including the house next door, in the early 1770s. The gable-roofed section is the older portion of the shop. Despite a late nineteenth-century facade and earlier additions to the rear, the original shop had remained essentially intact when restoration of the building began in 1940.

143 Taliaferro-Cole House
Private

The western section of this house dates from coachmaker Charles Taliaferro's period of ownership, starting in the 1770s, but the restored house reflects its appearance as enlarged in the early 1800s. The house's garden, like many in the Historic Area, is a riot of color from spring through fall. The house was restored in 1941.

144 African American Religion Exhibit (Taliaferro-Cole Stable)
Open to the public

Near the intersection of Nassau and Francis Streets is an exhibit on the religious experience of African Americans in the eighteenth century. African American preachers included Moses, who is credited with establishing a church as early as 1776, and Gowan Pamphlet. Oral tradition suggests that, since patrols were on the lookout for secret gatherings of enslaved people, Pamphlet preached hidden in arbors made of saplings and underbrush several miles from town. Pamphlet was ultimately freed from slavery and in the 1790s oversaw the acceptance of his church into the general Baptist association. That church met in a wooden carriage house near the site of this exhibit, and the congregation still meets as the First Baptist Church a few blocks away on Scotland Street.

The stable was part of the Taliaferro-Cole property in the 1760s and burned in 1771. It was reconstructed in 1941.

145 Bowden-Armistead House
Private

Completed in 1858, this house is an example of Greek Revival architecture. The Colonial Williamsburg Foundation does not own it.

146 Bryan House
Private

By the late 1700s, a house existed where this one now stands. It survived until early in the twentieth century. In reconstructing the gable-roofed house in 1942, architects were guided by photographs and recollections of Williamsburg residents as well as archaeological records. The parterres in the garden are based on patterns depicted on eighteenth-century maps of North Carolina towns.

147 Catherine Blaikley House
Private

Catherine Blaikley, who lived on this property until her death in 1771, was renowned as an "eminent Midwife . . . who, in the Course of her Practice, brought upwards of three Thousand Children into the World." A substantial building with three rooms on the ground floor was standing here by 1736. The house was reconstructed in 1952.

148 Tailor (Durfey Shop)
Open to ticket holders

Tailors in eighteenth-century America cut and constructed clothing for citizens of every station: the gentleman's fine suit, the lady's practical riding habit, the enslaved laborer's humble jacket and trousers were all made-to-order. Customers often brought fabrics and trims to the tailor, having purchased them from merchants throughout town. A few merchant-tailors, such as Robert Nicolson and Severinus Durfey, offered a broad choice in materials as well as their tailoring skills. On the eve of the Revolution, a dozen or more tailor shops were scattered throughout Williamsburg, many of which were busy making uniforms and tents for Virginia's new army.

Today, Colonial Williamsburg's tailors practice and preserve the trade on the spot where Severinus Durfey was working by 1773. The shop was reconstructed in 1952. Nicolson's original store, not open to the public, still stands near the Pasteur & Galt Apothecary Shop.

149, 150 John Blair House and Kitchen
Private

This house is one of the oldest in Williamsburg. The original, easterly part was built in 1720–1723. The house is named for its early owner, John Blair Sr., a nephew of the Reverend James Blair, minister of Bruton Parish Church and first president of the College of William & Mary. John Blair Sr. twice served as acting governor of the colony. His son signed the US Constitution and served on the Supreme Court. The house was restored in 1929. The parterres in the garden are planted with herbs that Virginians used for their scents. Some made the house smell sweeter, some added fragrance to perfumes and wigs, some scented fabrics, and some repelled bugs.

Francis Street

151 Custis Kitchen
Private
This building, in a field near the corner of Francis and Nassau Streets, is the sole survivor of a series of remarkable buildings and landscape owned by John Custis, best known as the first husband of Martha Washington. Custis settled in Williamsburg about 1715 and built a substantial brick house and a number of outbuildings. This structure was built in the early nineteenth century, replacing the original kitchen. It later became part of the sprawling grounds of Eastern State Hospital, which converted it to a storage building. It has not been restored.

152 Public Hospital of 1773
Open to ticket holders
The Public Hospital was the first public institution in British North America devoted exclusively to the care and treatment of individuals with mental disorders. Governor Francis Fauquier proposed establishing the hospital in 1766, and it opened in 1773. After a fire destroyed the building in 1885, the facility was rebuilt. In the mid-1960s, the hospital, which had expanded to form a sizable campus, was moved to the outskirts of Williamsburg, and the buildings were torn down. The structure was reconstructed on its original site in 1985 following the form and details of the original building. It includes cells that show the evolution of the treatments for mental illness.

153 Travis House
Private
Burgess Edward Champion Travis built the western portion of this house between 1762 and 1765. Sometime later a second room was built, and then in 1794–1795 a third. At the beginning of the restoration, Colonial Williamsburg moved the house to the south side of Duke of Gloucester Street opposite Palace Green and opened it as a restaurant. The building was later moved back to its present location on its original foundations. Its restoration was completed in 1930.

THE ENTIRE HISTORIC AREA is a museum. The buildings, their furnishings, and their environs are themselves museum "pieces," and most of the buildings contain actual antiques from the colonial period. But the exhibition buildings cannot safely or accurately house all of the original furnishings, artwork, ceramics, textiles, and more that Colonial Williamsburg has collected over the decades. The Foundation's collections include nearly seventy thousand examples of American and British fine, decorative, and mechanical art; seven thousand pieces of American folk art; more than sixty million archaeological artifacts; and fifteen thousand architectural fragments.

To most fully appreciate what life was like in early America, you will want to see more of the original items from the period and discover the stories behind them. Many of the pieces at the DeWitt Wallace Decorative Arts Museum are masterworks by famous artists and artisans of the period. But works by lesser-known crafts-people, even pieces as small as a once

commonplace pot or pistol, can reveal much about the lives of people in the colonial, Revolutionary, and early national periods.

You'll also want to visit the Abby Aldrich Rockefeller Folk Art Museum to see one of the nation's premiere collections of work by American painters, potters, quilters, woodworkers, and metalsmiths and other talented men and women working outside the mainstream of formal training.

A $42 million expansion of the museums means 165,000 square feet, including new gallery spaces and a grand new entrance with a spacious lobby and portals into both the DeWitt Wallace and the Abby Aldrich Rockefeller Folk Art Museum. There's also more space for the programs and activities as well as for the café and museum store.

The museums also regularly feature an array of programs such as lectures and panel discussions, dramatic and musical performances, hands-on craft activities, family programs, children's activities, and murder mystery tours.

DeWitt Wallace Decorative Arts Museum

Objects from the decorative arts collection furnish more than two hundred rooms in the Historic Area, but many of the most remarkable are displayed in the DeWitt Wallace Museum. You can see what was made here in Williamsburg and how and why it was used. You can also see masterworks by artists such as Charles Willson Peale. Both long-term and changing exhibitions illuminate life in Virginia and America before, during, and after the Revolution.

The DeWitt Wallace Decorative Arts Museum displays an extensive collection of American and British antiques, including furniture, metals, ceramics, glass, paintings, prints, firearms, and textiles from the seventeenth, eighteenth, and nineteenth centuries.

A small sampling follows.

1816 Grand Piano
Grand Piano, William Stodart, London, England, 1816, gift of Irene Bernard Hilliard

The piano was purchased by the wealthy Richmond, Virginia, merchant Thomas Rutherford for his daughter Jane Rutherford Meade. It probably was supplied by Adam Stodart, a Richmond musical instrument dealer and a relative of the piano maker. Adam Stodart is known to have imported pianos made by his London relatives William and Matthew Stodart.

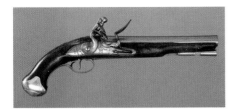

Light Dragoon Pistol

Pattern 1759 Elliot Light Dragoon Pistol, Board of Ordnance, London or Birmingham, England, 1760–1764

The Pattern 1759 pistol was developed for use by the newly raised regiments of British Light Dragoons during the French and Indian War. During the American Revolution, it was one of the most common pistols carried by troops fighting on both sides. One of many in Colonial Williamsburg's collection, this example was once part of an arms display at Stirling Castle, Scotland.

Silver Cream Pot

Cream Pot, Alexander Young, Camden, South Carolina, 1820–1830

British troops burned most of Camden, South Carolina, in 1781, but it was rebuilt and rose to prominence in the postwar years due largely to shipping on the Wateree River. Alexander Young appears to have been the city's most prolific silversmith in the postwar era. Born in Scotland, he trained in Baltimore prior to settling in Camden by 1807. This cream pot bearing his mark is notable for its unusual patterns of milled banding and its winged animal-paw feet.

South Carolina Chest

Double Chest of Drawers, Charleston, South Carolina, 1765–1780

During the second half of the eighteenth century, the double chest of drawers was the most popular form for clothing and textile storage in elite Lowcountry (coastal South Carolina) households. It became fashionable in Britain about midcentury, which likely accounts for its almost immediate acceptance in the Anglocentric Lowcountry. The simplest Charleston-made double chests feature a flat top with a simple cornice, but other options were available at additional cost. With its enriched cornice, ornate pediment, and secretary (desk) drawer, this example is the finest of the known survivors.

Peale's Portrait of Washington

Portrait of George Washington, Charles Willson Peale, Philadelphia, Pennsylvania, 1780, gift of John D. Rockefeller Jr.

On January 18, 1779, the Supreme Executive Council of Pennsylvania, "Deeply sensible how much the liberty, safety, & happiness of America . . . is owing to His Excell'y General Washington," requested that the commander sit for painter Charles Willson Peale for a portrait. Washington complied in late January.

Peale began receiving requests for replicas even before he completed the original. He varied the replicas, placing the commander variously on the battlefield of Princeton, Trenton, or Yorktown. Eight full-length versions are known to survive.

Peale used a state portrait formula in posing Washington, echoing the stance of George III in Allan Ramsay's coronation portrait of the British monarch, creating a statement that was satiric as well as earnest. Could anyone viewing Peale's painting doubt that America possessed heroic leaders on par with Europe's?

Ceremonial Armchair and Matching Back Stool

Governor's Chair (left) and Back Stool (right), England, ca. 1750, Museum Purchase, the Friends of Colonial Williamsburg Collections Fund, and the TIF Foundation in memory of Michelle A. Iverson

This impressive ceremonial armchair and matching back stool were part of a suite that included a matching footstool and at least twelve back stools. The furniture must have been ordered from England around 1750 for use in the Council Chamber of Virginia's Capitol. The Council, consisting of twelve elite Virginians, met in the chamber to advise the governor on matters affecting the entire colony. As befit their position in society and government, these councillors sat in very expensive chairs made of highly carved tropical mahogany upholstered in red silk and adorned with polished brass tacks. Seating this costly was rarely seen in Virginia.

Glass Dessert Stand

Sweetmeat Stand, England, 1760–1765, gift of John V. Rowan Jr. in memory of Winifred Draco Shrubsole

This stand is a remarkably complete example of the most elaborate type of dessert glassware. Its components would have been filled with nuts and sweetmeats (candied fruits). The cut glass and gilded metal mounts were designed to reflect the glow of candlelight, further enhancing the sparkling appearance of the whole. Although now rare, glass sweetmeat stands once graced the dessert tables of many prominent colonial families, including those of George Washington, John Randolph, and John Marshall.

Early Map of the Chesapeake Bay and Environs

A Map of the Most Inhabited Part of Virginia Containing the Whole Province of Maryland with Part of Pensilvania, New Jersey and North Carolina, engraved by Thomas Jefferys after Joshua Fry and Peter Jefferson, London, England, 1768

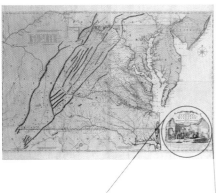

In Virginia and Maryland, the Chesapeake Bay and its tributaries were the single most important factor in shaping the culture. Thousands of miles of waterfront provided rich land well suited for an agrarian economy supported by slave labor. The wealthiest colonists amassed large plantations along the shorelines. These waterways were critical to the tobacco trade, allowing ships to sail inland for miles to load tobacco directly at each plantation. This advantage spared planters the expense of transporting their crops over land.

The connection between the landscape and the slave-based economy was made clear in the cartouche of this map. The seated planter, being served a drink, is the only one for whom a chair was provided. The standing man in the foreground is presumably the ship captain. The scantily clothed laborers working in the background represent the labor force necessary for tobacco cultivation. The enslaved were depicted in a subservient manner.

Silver-Plate Turtle Soup Tureen
Soup Tureen, probably Sheffield, England, ca. 1815, bequest of Dr. Lowry Dale Kirby

The technique of fusing silver to copper was developed in Sheffield, England, in 1742. Known as Sheffield plate, this new metal rapidly attained popularity at home and abroad because of its success in mimicking sterling silver at a lower cost. Manufacturers offered a wide array of forms in silver plate, from candlesticks to tableware. This tureen provided its owner with a fanciful means of serving turtle soup, a popular and costly dish that might have been the first setting at a dinner.

Massachusetts Sampler
Sampler, Mary Welsh, Massachusetts, ca. 1770

Characteristic of Boston samplers worked between 1760 and 1790, this one features a reclining shepherdess, male "pole vaulter," spotted black dog, and trio of sheep—two white and one black—motifs typically found on "fishing lady" pictures, so-called because the dominant figure is of a lady fishing.

Despite their obvious complexity, most early American and British samplers were fabricated by young girls as a part of their education for "housewifery." This sampler is signed "Mary Welsh Her Sampler Wrought in the 12 Year of Her Age."

Tall Case Clock
Tall Case Clock, attributed to Peter Rife and David Whipple, Pulaski County, Virginia, ca. 1810

Visually arresting, this clock is distinguished by great height and an ambitious combination of Germanic inlays, brass and silver mounts, and projecting ornaments. Sebastian Wygal of Montgomery (now Pulaski) County in southwestern Virginia likely acquired it about 1810. The case was probably fashioned by cabinetmaker Peter Rife, who was born in Rockland Township, Pennsylvania, and resided in southwestern Virginia by the 1770s. David Whipple signed the movement in a closely related clock. He was married to Wygal's niece.

Cherokee Chief in London

Cunne Shote, the Indian Chief, a Great Warrior of the Cherokee Nation, engraved by James McArdell after Francis Parsons, London, England, ca. 1763

Cunne Shote was one of the three Cherokee men escorted to London in 1762 by Henry Timberlake, a British officer who had lived with the Cherokee. While in London, Cunne Shote sat for an oil portrait that was subsequently engraved in mezzotint.

Cunne Shote's combination of English and Native clothing and accoutrements was meant to suggest harmony between cultures. The medals around his neck commemorate the marriage of George III and Charlotte of Mecklenburg while the crescent-shaped silver gorget bears the initials "GR III." The forceful grip that Cunne Shote has on the scalping knife, however, is a reminder of the tenuous relationship between the Cherokees and the European settlers.

Pierced Stoneware

Gorge, James Morley, Nottingham, England, ca. 1700
This finely carved gorge is attributed to James Morley's pottery. Similar wares appear on a trade card issued by Morley around 1700. The gorge is constructed as a double-walled vessel with foliate piercing cut through the outer wall. The technique, which demands considerable skill, may be derived from Chinese porcelain decorated in the so-called Ling Lung method of pierced decoration.

Engraved Pewter Dish

Dish, John Townsend and Thomas Giffin, London, England, 1768–1778
This dish was boldly decorated in 1782 for Hanna Feeshel of Shepherdstown, Virginia (now West Virginia). The nature of the ornament and the use of hammer engraving strongly suggest that a local gunsmith augmented this dish, transforming a plain English vessel into a highly individual serving piece. Gunsmiths were probably among the few in that area who had the requisite engraving skills.

Abby Aldrich Rockefeller Folk Art Museum

Folk artists use bold colors, simplified shapes, and imaginative surface patterns to create a variety of engaging paintings, carvings, furniture, metalware, ceramics, quilts, needlework, and toys. The Abby Aldrich Rockefeller Folk Art Museum—the nation's oldest institution dedicated to the study and preservation of such material—houses some seven thousand treasures, a sampling of which follows. The collection grew from an important assemblage of folk art that pioneering collector Abby Aldrich Rockefeller gave to Colonial Williamsburg in 1939. It is not limited to early works but rather includes material from the eighteenth century to the present.

African American Life
The Old Plantation, attributed to John Rose, Beaufort County, South Carolina, 1785–1790, gift of Abby Aldrich Rockefeller

Arguably the best-known depiction of slaves in eighteenth-century America, *The Old Plantation* is remarkable for its sensitive, highly individualized depictions of enslaved men and women and for recording their efforts to maintain African cultural traditions in the context of plantation life. Depicted is a West African stick dance performed to the accompaniment of several African musical instruments. The setting is likely artist John Rose's plantation about ten miles from Beaufort, South Carolina. Rose was educated in the classics, music, and art and devoted his free time to artistic pursuits.

Pictorial Signboard
Eagle Signboard, New England, 1821–1841, gift of Juli Grainger

Nineteenth-century signboards often combined symbols and texts, but many lacked wording. Pictorial signage could be quite effective. Anyone seeking this proprietor's services would have been directed to "the sign of the eagle." A spread eagle bearing a striped shield was the central motif of the Great Seal of the United States, adopted in 1782. Rapidly thereafter, the image gained recognition as a symbol of the new nation. As in many cases, the eagle here is surrounded by thirteen stars.

Painted Chest
Blanket Chest, attributed to Johannes Spitler, Shenandoah (now Page) County, Virginia, 1800–1805

During the late eighteenth and early nineteenth centuries, furniture painter Johannes Spitler worked in the Shenandoah Valley, where isolation facilitated the preservation of distinctive northern European cultural traditions. Using brilliant, saturated colors, he painted chests, clock cases, and other forms with symbol-laden ornament that reflected his Swiss- and German-American heritage. The stylized birds, hearts, vines, and flowers signify a range of themes, including abundance, faith, love, fecundity, and spiritual growth.

Portrait of Baby
Baby in Red Chair, America, 1810–1830, collection of Abby Aldrich Rockefeller, gift of David Rockefeller

This endearing portrait was among the earliest acquisitions of pioneering folk art collector Abby Aldrich Rockefeller. Today, it is a favorite of visitors to the museum named by her husband in her memory. The infant's innocence, contentment, and lack of self-consciousness seldom fail to elicit smiles from viewers. The sleeping baby appears oblivious to the world around, comforted and cradled by a soft white pillow and secure in the protective embrace of a sturdy, child-size armchair.

Baltimore Album Quilt
Baltimore Album Quilt, Sarah Anne Whittington Lankford, Baltimore, Maryland, 1847–1853, gift of Marsha C. Scott

Like other album quilts made in and near Baltimore, this one consists of elaborate blocks of appliquéd wreaths, baskets, and urns, in addition to buildings and monuments. The second block in the top row depicts a memorial tribute to Major Samuel Ringgold, a Maryland soldier who died in the Battle of Palo Alto, the first engagement of the Mexican-American War. According to family tradition, Henry Smith Lankford purchased the professionally made squares at a Baltimore auction, and they were assembled and quilted by his sister, Sarah Anne Whittington Lankford.

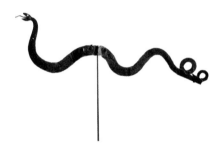

Serpent Weather Vane
Weather Vane, New England, ca. 1850, gift of Abby Aldrich Rockefeller

This snake's gaping mouth, serrated teeth, and ominous tongue perpetuate the image of serpents as venomous aggressors. But the silhouette's rhythmic grace and sinuous beauty contrast markedly with that stereotype. Minute details of this vane, such as the teeth, the twisted-wire tongue, and the carefully placed eye are unusual considering that weather vanes were typically placed some distance from the viewer, often rendering such details indiscernible. The maker's skill at working iron and the pleasure taken in designing and fabricating the piece apparently outweighed such considerations.

Sculpture of Young Child
Portrait of Amanda Clayanna Armstrong, Asa Ames, Evans, New York, 1847, gift of Barbara Rice in memory of her grandfather Arthur T. White and her mother, Eleanor Rice

Asa Ames carved this portrait when his subject was three and a half years old. The informality of Amanda's pose is perfectly suited to a child's likeness. It also shows how little Ames was influenced by the theatrical attitudes in which high-style sculptors depicted their subjects. Amanda's attire is also realistic. Rather than presenting her in flowing neo-classical drapery, Ames showed her wearing what was, most likely, her own fashionable late-1840s frock. The familiar costume, Amanda's relaxed stance, and her outstretched hand provide a degree of spontaneity not seen in more academic likenesses. Besides being an exceptional achievement for a carver who was barely twenty-three years old, the sculpture reminds us of the importance Americans attached to images of children at a time when infant mortality rates were high.

Peaceable Kingdom

Peaceable Kingdom, Edward Hicks, Bucks County, Pennsylvania, 1832–1834, collection of Abby Aldrich Rockefeller, gift of David Rockefeller

During a career of nearly four decades, Edward Hicks painted more than five dozen versions of the Peaceable Kingdom. He gradually varied his pictorial interpretations of Isaiah 11:6–9 to reflect his personal struggles with Quaker theology and especially his deep anguish over the sect's split into Hicksite and Orthodox believers. Hicks's distress can be read in the evolving positions and facial expressions of the animals and in the overall composition.

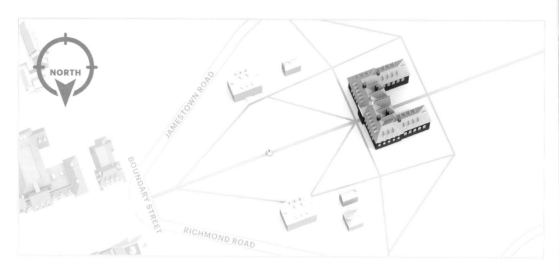

The College of William & Mary

The oldest academic structure in English-speaking America, the **Wren Building** is still used by the College of William & Mary, which is the second oldest institution of higher education—after Harvard University—in the United States. The college received a charter from King William and Queen Mary in 1693, and construction of the building began two years later. Thomas Jefferson, James Monroe, and John Marshall were among those who studied in the building.

The building bears the name of the distinguished English architect Sir Christopher Wren, who is erroneously credited with its original design. Three times damaged by fire, the building has often changed in appearance. Restored in 1928–1931, it was the first major structure completed by Colonial Williamsburg and today looks much as it did in 1732.

Located on the north side of the college yard, the **President's House** was built in 1732–1733. Restored in 1931, it still serves its original function as the official residence of the institution's president.

On the south side of the college yard, the **Brafferton** was constructed in 1723 to house the college's school for Native American boys. Restored in 1932, it currently houses college offices.

The Brafferton building
at William & Mary

Colonial Williamsburg: The Guide

Colonial Parkway

Jamestown and Yorktown

Linked by the scenic twenty-three-mile Colonial Parkway, the three points of America's Historic Triangle—Jamestown, Williamsburg, and Yorktown—each played a crucial role in the nation's journey to liberty and independence.

Jamestown

In 1607, three ships carrying 104 people arrived at what they would call Jamestown and what would become the first lasting English settlement in America. Twelve years later, the first elected assembly in English North America convened in Jamestown, a crucial step towards democracy. That same year, a ship carried to Virginia the first enslaved Africans to land on the mainland of English America.

Historic Jamestowne encompasses the island where the settlers first landed. You can see where archaeologists excavated the 1607 James Fort: palisades have been reconstructed above the original remains. At the Nathalie P. and Alan M. Voorhees Archaearium, you can examine some of the artifacts archaeologists uncovered and better understand what they reveal about the settlers and the extreme hardships they withstood. The National Park Service and Preservation Virginia jointly administer Historic Jamestowne.

At **Jamestown Settlement**, on the mainland just before the island, you can board replicas of the ships that carried the settlers to the New World and explore re-creations of a 1610 fort and a Powhatan Indian village. Indoor galleries chronicle the cultures of the Indians, the Europeans, and the Africans that converged here. Jamestown Settlement is operated by the Commonwealth of Virginia.

Yorktown

The last great battle of the American Revolution took place at Yorktown. In 1781, General George Washington's troops, aided by French allies, defeated British troops and assured American independence.

At the Visitor Center of the **Yorktown Battlefield**, you can see a film about the siege of Yorktown, and you can view artifacts from the siege. Outside, you can walk around the battlefield or take a seven-mile self-guided driving tour along American and French siege lines and see where the surrender took place. The National Park Service administers Yorktown Battlefield.

The village of Yorktown includes a mix of historic sites and private residences and buildings. On the other side of the town from the battlefield, the **American Revolution Museum at Yorktown**, operated by the Commonwealth of Virginia, has indoor and outdoor exhibits.

STAY, DINE, SHOP ▲▲

Accommodations

GUESTS WHO STAY AT AN official Colonial Williamsburg hotel receive discounts on admission tickets and passes; unlimited use of the Colonial Williamsburg shuttle buses; and preferred reservations for spa services, dining, tennis courts, and tee times for golf. Colonial Williamsburg Resorts offers a range of accommodations including the luxury of the Forbes Travel Guide Five-Star and AAA Five-Diamond Williamsburg Inn, the newly renovated Williamsburg Lodge–Autograph Collection, the Colonial Houses–Historic Lodging, the Griffin Hotel, and the family-friendly Williamsburg Woodlands Hotel & Suites adjacent to the Visitor Center. For reservations and hotel package information, call 855-368-3287 or visit colonialwilliamsburg.org.

Williamsburg Inn

The Williamsburg Inn, the landmark property conceived by John D. Rockefeller Jr. and opened in April 1937, has been the crown jewel of Williamsburg for more than eighty years. Under the direction of renowned Boston architect William Perry, the Inn was designed and decorated in the Regency style of nineteenth-century England, giving it

a style very distinct from the colonial architecture in the Historic Area.

The Inn's striking whitewashed brick facade is marked by a generous balcony with tall Ionic columns, wrought-iron railings, and a graceful arched portico entrance. The Regency style is evident in neoclassical architectural features ranging from interior cornices and chair rails to the exterior pediments, arches, and columns. Guest rooms are exquisitely and individually decorated.

Four themed luxury suites are named for John D. Rockefeller Jr., Queen Elizabeth II, Winston Churchill, and Forrest Mars. Each left a mark on Williamsburg. And each suite has a unique ambience and iconic photographs from the person's time in Williamsburg. All rooms feature period furnishings of Honduras mahogany and handmade silk window treatments, a Williamsburg Inn signature.

Rooms offer views of the golf course, gardens, and new social terrace. Some feature canopy beds with separate sitting areas and wood-burning fireplaces. Spacious bathrooms feature twin marble vanities, Italian marble–enclosed soaking tubs, and large marble showers.

While the rooms are rich in history, hotel amenities address the needs of today's travelers. If he were alive today, Rockefeller would surely applaud the addition of spacious writing desks and delight in the concierge staff, twenty-four-hour room service, and wireless internet connectivity. Inn guests have access to one indoor and two outdoor pools and the fitness center at the Spa of Colonial Williamsburg.

Nestled on the Inn's grounds is the Griffin Hotel, featuring large contemporary accommodations with breezy balconies in a garden setting. Some rooms include a fireplace and overlook a fountain pond.

The Williamsburg Inn's culinary team serves the sophisticated Rockefeller Room and beautiful patio known as the Social Terrace, the refined Terrace Room, and the Goodwin Room. The Inn's history includes a succession of masterful chefs who have delighted heads of state, celebrities, VIPs, and guests who return time after time to celebrate special occasions or simply enjoy meals that celebrate the heritage of the Chesapeake Bay area and embrace international tastes.

The Rockefeller Room is the Inn's signature contemporary fine-dining experience. The Terrace Room is the perfect retreat for lunch, cocktails, hors d'oeuvres, and a light dinner. The Social Terrace offers alfresco dining and breathtaking views and is the spot to enjoy signature cocktails complemented by a variety of small plates. Guests are encouraged to stop by to socialize.

The elegant Regency Room looks out onto the resort's world-class golf course and serves as a private venue for meetings, conferences, corporate events, weddings, and family reunions.

Williamsburg Lodge, Autograph Collection

Opened in 1939, the Williamsburg Lodge was, like the Inn, con-structed under the guidance of John D. Rockefeller Jr., the first bene-factor of the town's restoration. From the original bluestone floors to the cypress accents and eighteenth-century inspirations, in every cozy nook and spacious expanse, the Williamsburg Lodge reflects its Virginia heritage.

With its 11,200-square-foot Virginia Room and 45,000 square feet of meeting and banquet space, the Lodge is a premier conference choice in the mid-Atlantic and a prime location for meetings, ban-quets, and weddings as well as for a family vacation or couple's get-away. All guests receive a generous helping of Southern hospitality, impeccable service, and amenities including access to the fitness center at the Spa of Colonial Williamsburg, two outdoor pools, and one indoor lap pool. The Lodge is fully Wi-Fi capable, and a business center provides a fax, computer, and printer.

The 323 recently renovated guest rooms have furnishings inspired by the objects, stories, and architecture of Colonial Williamsburg. Four guesthouses—the Ashby and Custis houses, with thirty rooms each, and the Nicholas and Tyler houses, with thirty-eight rooms each—complement the renovated South Hall and Tazewell guest rooms. The entire Lodge complex is connected by a series of covered walkways.

The culinary team at the Lodge's Traditions dining room has created innovative menus that are an ode to the bounty of Virginia with local oysters, beef and pork from regional farms, and seasonal vegetables. Always in season are Virginia wines. Sweet Tea & Barley offers down-home flavors—you'll find handcrafted cocktails, cuisine, and service.

Colonial Houses–Historic Lodging

Located throughout the Historic Area, Colonial Houses combine eighteenth-century charm with twenty-first-century resort amenities. Guests can wake up to the sound of sheep in a pasture, take a morning walk on Duke of Gloucester Street, enjoy spa services or golf, and return to a wood fire and a tavern dinner. The lodgings range from a room in a tavern to a full house with multiple bedrooms or a tiny eighteenth-century dependency that might have been a detached kitchen or laundry. Each house is furnished with period reproductions. Some have canopy beds, some have working fireplaces, and some overlook private gardens.

Williamsburg Woodlands Hotel & Suites

The Williamsburg Woodlands Hotel & Suites is the spot for an old-fashioned getaway, business conference, or family vacation. The contemporary, three-story hotel offers 96 suites and 202 guest rooms, all accessed from secure, interior hallways. The hotel features a spacious lobby bathed in natural light from cathedral ceiling skylights. A hospitality suite just off the lobby provides an informal gathering spot.

Guest rooms each have two full-size beds, a sitting area with a desk and two chairs, a coffeepot, a comfortable lounge chair (that converts to a single bed), and cable television. Each suite has a sitting room with queen sofa bed, desk, and cable television as well as a counter with a small refrigerator, microwave, sink, and coffeemaker; the separate bedroom has a king-size bed and second television. A traditional continental breakfast is served daily.

Recreational options include a heated pool open from March to October and an adjacent splash zone with interactive water toys, cascading canoes and barrels, and geysers. During the summer months, a poolside snack bar open in the evenings serves drinks, snacks, and sandwiches. Miniature golf, table tennis, volleyball, shuffleboard, storytelling around the firepit, pool parties, and games round out the fun.

Huzzah's Eatery, across the promenade from the hotel, is a family-friendly restaurant where kids can create their own pizzas. All selections on the menu are made from scratch, including the barbecue sauces. Outdoor seating is available, and the full-service bar is a great spot to watch sports. Huzzah's is open for breakfast and dinner.

Recreation

Resort Golf

The Golden Horseshoe Golf Club includes forty-five holes on three courses. Designed by the legendary Robert Trent Jones Sr., the Gold Course, located behind the Williamsburg Inn, is one of the best examples of traditional golf course architecture in the world. The course is a Certified Audubon Cooperative Sanctuary and has been named one of *Golf Magazine*'s Top 100 You Can Play, *Golf Digest*'s 75 Best Golf Resorts in North America and America's 100 Greatest Public Courses, and *Golfweek*'s Best Resort Courses.

Jones Sr. called the Gold Course, opened in 1963, his "finest design." In 1998, Rees Jones, Jones Sr.'s son, was the architect of a course renovation that remained faithful to the original design but expanded the appeal of the course for higher-handicap players while lengthening the course from the back tees. The Gold Course underwent a full-scale restoration in 2017, regrassing all surfaces with the latest in turf and rebuilding every bunker.

Rees Jones designed the Green Course, which opened in 1991 and has been acclaimed by national and regional golf magazines. The

layout is carved from the same terrain as the Gold Course and is more typical of contemporary trends in golf course architecture. The two courses are the first father-son tandem of side-by-side layouts.

Named for colonial governor Alexander Spotswood, the nine-hole Spotswood Course is the elder Jones's 1964 update of the Williamsburg Inn's original 1947 nine-hole course. *Golf Magazine* called it the "best 9-hole short course in the country."

The Golden Horseshoe Gold Course Clubhouse Grill offers casual dining overlooking a tranquil pond and the serene finish of the eighteenth hole while the Golden Horseshoe Green Course Clubhouse Grill provides a sweeping view of the amphitheater eighteenth finish. Menus include sandwiches, wraps, salads, desserts, and cocktails. Shops at both courses offer all your golfing essentials from leading vendors including Ping, Titleist, Callaway, Ahead, Maui Jim, and TaylorMade alongside unique logo tumblers, wine glasses, and wallets. The shops are the exclusive outlet for Golden Horseshoe apparel with top brands such as Peter Millar, FootJoy, TravisMathew, Adidas, and more. William & Mary co-branded items are also available. The Golden Horseshoe Golf Club is open to the public and also offers memberships, tournaments, and instruction for juniors and adults.

For information and to reserve tee times, call 757-220-7696.

What was "THE GOLDEN HORSESHOE"?

Daring adventures are part of Virginia's history, but few are as significant as Governor Alexander Spotswood's 1716 expedition to explore the far reaches of the colony of Virginia. Spotswood, aware of the frontier's economic potential and bent on encouraging westward settlement, led a party of sixty-three men on the arduous journey.

In *The Present State of Virginia,* published in London in 1724, Hugh Jones offered his account of the toll taken by the rocky soil of the Piedmont and the Blue Ridge: "For this Expedition they were obliged to provide a great Quantity of Horse-Shoes; (Things seldom used in the lower Parts of the Country, where there are few Stones:) ... the Governor upon their Return presented each of his Companions with a Golden Horse-Shoe, (some of which I have seen studded with valuable Stones resembling the Heads of Nails)." The recipients became known as the Knights of the Golden Horseshoe. Although several people in the nineteenth century claimed to have seen them, none of the small, golden horseshoes described by Jones have been found.

Spa

At the Spa of Colonial Williamsburg, you will find a complete array of traditional spa services as well as a full-service salon offering hair, nail, makeup, and depilatory (hair-removal) services. The Spa also has a large retail boutique and gender-specific locker rooms with amenities that include large whirlpools, eucalyptus steam rooms, cold plunge pool/shower, rain showers, ADA access, a lounge area, and signature Spa bathing amenities.

The twenty-thousand-square-foot facility is located between the Williamsburg Inn and the Williamsburg Lodge. It has twelve treatment rooms that include two couple's suites and three dedicated facial rooms. Additionally, there are three relaxation rooms (male, female, and coed/dining area). Spa dining is provided by the Williamsburg Inn.

The Spa also has a large state-of-the-art fitness center with all new strength equipment and treadmills introduced in 2017 and a sizable group fitness room with class offerings seven days a week. The fitness center is available to members and guests of the Inn and Lodge. Additionally, the Spa has three pools: one indoor heated lap pool and two outdoor pools. The West Pool (a.k.a. the Family Pool) is also heated. The East Pool (a.k.a. the Tranquility Pool), which offers a more restful setting, is not heated. There is a small dining area with a lite-fare menu provided by the Williamsburg Inn.

The Spa is also available for bridal services, "spa'rties," and group conference services.

Explore the spa and lifestyle boutique, which offers a variety of gifts and wellness and skin care products, including the Spa's signature lemongrass and lavender body care collection. Also available are clothing and workout wear from TravisMathew and Beyond Yoga, Helen Jon swimwear, and the coziest loungewear from P.J. Salvage. Discover the latest trends in powder, mascara, eye shadow, lip color, and more with makeup from Make up Factory.

The Spa of Colonial Williamsburg, which currently boasts a Forbes four-star rating, is open seven days a week. Call 757-220-7720.

Swimming and Fitness

Guests of the Inn, Lodge, Griffin Hotel, and Colonial Houses have complimentary access to the swimming pools and the fitness center at the Spa of Colonial Williamsburg. Guests of the Williamsburg Woodlands Hotel & Suites have a pool and a fitness center on location.

Walking and Biking

Colonial Williamsburg is a delight for walkers and bikers. The Historic Area offers one of the most picturesque locations in America for a brisk walk or a leisurely stroll. The 1.4-mile Bassett Trace Nature Trail starts at the Griffin Hotel.

Tennis

Players can enjoy six Har-Tru clay and two Premier Court surfaces at the Williamsburg Inn Tennis Club, located on the grounds in front of the Griffin Hotel. The full-service pro shop features men's and women's tennis attire and offers racket stringing, equipment rentals, and changing facilities. Lessons are available for youths and adults.

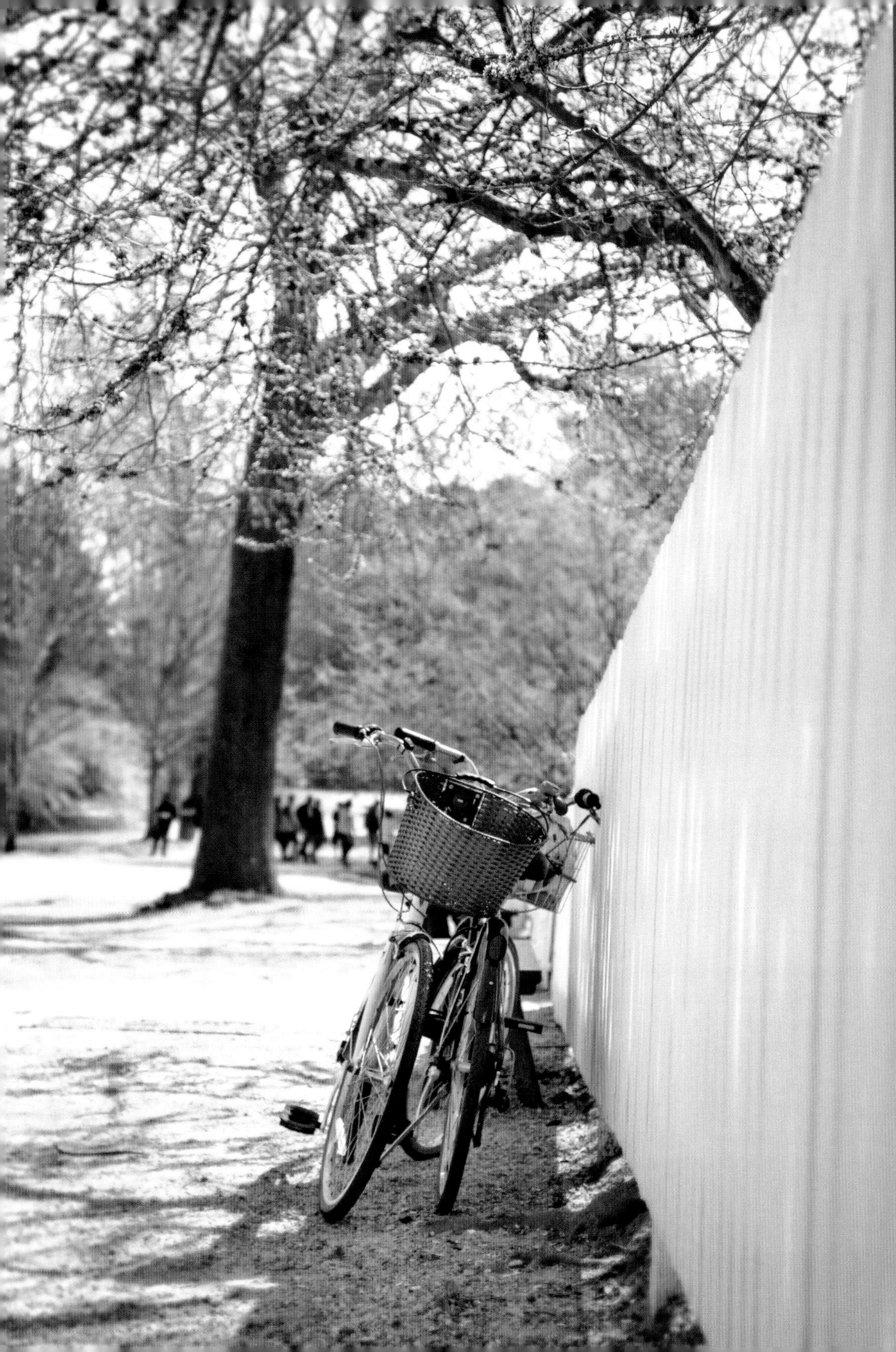

Colonial Williamsburg Dining

SCHEDULES AND MEALS served vary depending on the eatery and the season. Get up-to-date information at colonialwilliamsburg.org. Dinner reservations are recommended. Lunch reservations are available for groups of twenty or more. Call 855-368-3287.

Historic Dining Taverns

In the eighteenth century, taverns provided lodgings for travelers and served as community gathering places for meals, conversation, and entertainment. Today's tavern guests experience the flavor of the Revolution through atmosphere, entertainment, food, and beverages. The taverns offer craft beers, carefully selected wine pairings, foods prepared with fresh local ingredients, and specialty desserts.

Christiana Campbell's Tavern

George Washington loved the seafood in this tavern, and today's diners can savor vibrant seafood cuisine. Guests can enjoy a visit with Mrs. Campbell and sometimes the sounds of traveling musicians. *Capitol bus stop.*

Chowning's Tavern

This eighteenth-century alehouse features period-inspired foods and specialty brews. Dine inside or out under the grape arbor (weather permitting), and you may catch traveling musicians as well. *Magazine bus stop.*

King's Arms Tavern

The town's premier tavern offers a chophouse menu featuring Virginia's famous peanut soup, prime rib, pork chops, and game pye. Enjoy scheduled performances of popular music from the period. *Tavern bus stop.*

Shields Tavern

The menu at Shields reflects global influences, a reminder that

colonial Williamsburg was a port of call for ships from around the world. With gracious service, Shields Tavern offers a glimpse into the cosmopolitan nature of the British colonies. *Tavern bus stop.*

Other Historic Area Eateries

McKenzie Apothecary

On Palace Green next to the Robert Carter House, this quick stop offers snacks and beverages to warm or refresh. Refillable souvenir mugs are available for purchase. *Palace bus stop.*

M. Dubois Grocer

The grocer has Mars candy, fountain beverages, ice cream, and other sweet treats. Souvenir mugs can be purchased and refilled. *Tavern bus stop.*

Raleigh Tavern Bakery

The bakery has fresh sandwiches, salads, and baked treats along with hot and cold drinks. Souvenir mugs are sold and refilled. Casual seating is available in the courtyard and rear garden. *Tavern bus stop.*

Museum Café

Located in the Art Museums of Colonial Williamsburg, the café offers a light lunch, including soups, sandwiches, and freshly prepared desserts. *Museum bus stop.*

Other Colonial Williamsburg Restaurants

Golden Horseshoe Gold Course Clubhouse Grill

The Gold Course Clubhouse Grill, which overlooks the eighteenth green of Robert Trent Jones's famed Gold Course, offers sandwiches, salads, light entrées, desserts, and cocktails. *Williamsburg Lodge bus stop.*

Golden Horseshoe Green Course Clubhouse Grill

The Green Course Clubhouse Grill has a full lunch menu of favorites such as hot dogs, chicken tenders, salads, and appetizers.

Rockefeller Room in the Williamsburg Inn

The Inn's signature contemporary gourmet dining experience serves dinner featuring nouveau British cuisine with locally sourced ingredients. *Magazine bus stop.*

Terrace Room and Goodwin Room in the Williamsburg Inn

The Terrace Room and Goodwin Room offer guests the perfect retreat for breakfast, lunch, high tea, and a light dinner. *Magazine bus stop.*

Social Terrace at the Williamsburg Inn

Whether for a nightcap or to relax after a day of sightseeing, the Social Terrace is the spot to enjoy signature handcrafted cocktails complemented by a variety of small plates. *Magazine bus stop.*

Traditions at the Williamsburg Lodge

Using the freshest ingredients from the region, Traditions serves breakfast and lunch in the comfort and charm of the South. Wine Spectator Award of Excellence. *Williamsburg Lodge bus stop.*

Sweet Tea & Barley at the Williamsburg Lodge

Derived from artisanal spirits and sprinkled with the essence of Americana, the bar's libations and kitchen's home cooking are served day and night in a casual setting by the fireplace or in communal areas. Televisions available. Beverage and food specials. *Williamsburg Lodge bus stop.*

Cupboard Gourmet Grab & Go

Located inside the Williamsburg Lodge, the Cupboard offers tasty treats, refreshing beverages, and fresh coffee throughout the day. *Williamsburg Lodge bus stop.*

Huzzah's Eatery

Specializing in barbecued chicken, pork, and beef, Huzzah's also offers pizza and other favorites. Located on the promenade next to the Williamsburg Woodlands Hotel & Suites, steps from the Colonial Williamsburg Regional Visitor Center.

Visitor Center Café

In the Visitor Center next to WILLIAMSBURG Revolutions, the café has baked treats, fruit, sandwiches, and beverages. Souvenir mugs sold and refilled.

Merchants Square Dining

Aromas Coffee and Café
Gourmet coffee roasted on location, teas, smoothies, pastries, wine, and beer are served in the lively and welcoming atmosphere of an old world coffeehouse. Full breakfast, lunch, and dinner served daily. *757-221-6676*

Baskin-Robbins
Choose from a variety of ice creams, milkshakes, malts, sundaes, and frozen yogurt. Daily. *757-229-6385*

Berret's Restaurant and Taphouse Grill
Specializing in fresh regional seafood, Berret's has seasonal outdoor dining and live music. Lunch and dinner served daily. *757-253-1847*

Blackbird Bakery
Enjoy fresh baked goods from the kitchens of the Trellis Restaurant, Blue Talon Bistro, and DoG Street Pub, including yeast rolls, cinnamon sticky buns, fruit tarts, chocolate mousse, turtle bars, peanut butter pie, homemade granola, candies, and chocolate-covered coffee beans. Daily. *757-229-8610*

Blue Talon Bistro
Chef David Everett serves his "serious comfort food" in a relaxed bistro atmosphere. Intriguing wine list, Illy coffee. Breakfast, lunch, and dinner served daily. *757-476-BLUE*

The Cheese Shop
This Williamsburg institution offers two hundred imported and domestic cheeses, charcuterie, freshly baked breads, specialty foods, and more than four thousand bottles of wine in the wine cellar. Patio tables offer a relaxed setting to enjoy famous Cheese Shop sandwiches, a cheese plate, and a beer or glass of wine almost year-round. Daily. *757-220-1324*

DoG Street Pub
In this American gastropub, Chef David Everett delivers delicious food with American flair inspired by the uncomplicated dishes of an English pub. The pub features draft and bottled beers from around the globe in the relaxed setting of a neighborhood tavern. Outdoor dining in season. Lunch, dinner, and late-night dining served daily. *757-293-6478*

Fat Canary

Executive Chef Thomas Power Jr. is a graduate of the Culinary Institute of America. Since opening in 2003, the Fat Canary has earned awards and accolades for its innovative menu, service, and wine list. Reservations highly recommended. Dinner served daily. *757-229-3333*

Mellow Mushroom Pizza Bakers

For over forty years, Mellow Mushroom Pizza Bakers has been serving up fresh, stone-baked made-to-order pizzas and craft beer in an eclectic, art-filled, and family-friendly environment. Lunch and dinner served daily. *757-903-4762*

Precarious Beer Hall

The craft brewery Precarious Beer Project has found a home at Precarious Beer Hall, where you can taste small-batch beers in the tasting room and where the whole family can enjoy a street-style taqueria, vintage arcade games, live music, and ample outdoor seating. *757-808-5104*

The Trellis Restaurant

Chef David Everett offers contemporary American dining with a focus on local, responsibly raised products and small-scale artisan farmers to bring the best of the region's flavors to the table. Outdoor dining in season. Breakfast, lunch, and dinner served daily. *757-229-8610*

The Williamsburg Winery Tasting Room & Wine Bar

Guests can savor wine flights and wine by the glass or bottle in Williamsburg Winery's newly remodeled Tasting Room & Wine Bar or in its quaint outdoor wine garden. Cider, mead, and sparkling wine from around Virginia are also available. Daily. *757-229-0999*

COLONIAL WILLIAMSBURG OFFERS nearly six hundred items made in the USA—from glass stemware to Virginia peanuts to drums and sterling silver bracelets. WILLIAMSBURG products are available in retail stores located in Merchants Square, the Historic Area, the Visitor Center, the Williamsburg Lodge, and the Art Museums. Revenue from the sale of all products supports the restoration, preservation, and educational mission of The Colonial Williamsburg Foundation. Go to shop.colonialwilliamsburg.com or call 1-800-446-9240.

Colonial Williamsburg Shops

In the Historic Area

The Golden Ball
Fashionable, one-of-a-kind pieces of jewelry, including traditionally made accoutrements and bespoke pieces created by Colonial Williamsburg's own silversmiths just next door at James Craig Jeweller. Choose from earrings, pendants, charms, precious gemstone rings, and more.

John Greenhow Store
This is a traditional general store: Purchase fine imported porcelain, leather, pewter, tinware, food and drink, toiletries, and other essentials for your stroll through the Historic Area. Bring eighteenth-century charm into your kitchen with replica dinnerware from the King's Arms, Shields, Chowning's, and Christiana Campbell's Taverns. The shop also offers food, kitchen accessories, and floor coverings.

Market House
The commercial and social heart of the city, this open-air market sells in-season fruits and vegetables and a variety of fixings for a farm-fresh meal. These stands also sell toys, hats, pottery, and hand-crafted baskets.

Market House

Prentis Store

The Prentis Store showcases handcrafted items made by Colonial Williamsburg's tradespeople using eighteenth-century tools and techniques. Items include leather goods, iron hardware, tools, reproduction furniture, and pottery. Also available are men's colonial clothing, yarn from Colonial Williamsburg sheep, and Native American crafts.

Tarpley, Thompson & Company

Here you'll find eighteenth-century fashion for men, women, and children in the best of taste. Offerings include ready-made and made-to-order coats, waistcoats, breeches, petticoats, short gowns, cloaks, mitts, caps, beautifully decorated straw hats, and more—all made in Williamsburg. Complete your look with fashionable jewelry and ladies' toiletries.

William Pitt Store

Kids love browsing through this children's boutique. From eighteenth-century hats to toys, games, and books, the William Pitt Store offers a large selection of kid-friendly souvenirs, gifts, historic publications, and picture books. Get into the colonial spirit with eighteenth-century costume rentals for the whole family.

In the Visitor Center

WILLIAMSBURG Revolutions

WILLIAMSBURG Revolutions offers puzzles, games, toys, food, logo apparel, and more. Here you'll also find a bookshop with books for all ages as well as stationery and home and holiday decor. Take your visit to the next level with an eighteenth-century costume rental.

Other Colonial Williamsburg Shops

Museum Store

After discovering treasures from the past in the Art Museums of Colonial Williamsburg, pick up a treasure of your own. The Museum Store offers jewelry, needlework, books, and reproductions. Among the special finds are handmade pottery, glassware, and framed prints inspired by the folk art collection.

Williamsburg Lodge Gift Shop

Contemporary souvenirs, jewelry, personal accessories, and unique gifts are specialties of this boutique gift shop. Forgot something? Sundries and gourmet snacks are also available.

Spa Boutique

The Spa offers premium spa products and related goods, including robes, candles, skin and hair care products, and signature lavender, lemongrass, and colonial mint products.

Golden Horseshoe Gold Course Pro Shop

Golfers can choose from a wide selection of top golf equipment, custom and personalized golf bags, resort wear, and Golden Horseshoe logo apparel for ladies and men.

Golden Horseshoe Green Course Pro Shop

Golfing essentials, including custom and personalized golf bags, gloves, balls, hats, polo shirts, and footwear, are available in the pro shop at the Green Course.

Merchants Square Shops

Blink
Blink is your source for distinctive gifts, jewelry, art, and home accessories. The goal is to provide you with the unique and the surprisingly delightful. Interior design services are available. *757-645-2540*

Boxwood and Berry
A modern garden emporium awaits you with greenery and garden inspirations for all seasons. Casual furniture, lanterns, and more make great additions to your outdoor living space as well as gifts for the green thumb. Shop for an assortment of holiday decorations, entertaining essentials, and seasonal floral arrangements. *757-565-1710*

Campus Shop
This is Tribe headquarters for the College of William & Mary apparel and gifts. *757-229-4301*

The Carousel Children's Clothier
This shop carries classic children's clothing and accessories. *757-229-1710*

Chico's
Women can find everything from casual clothing to elegant evening wear in this nationally known shop. *757-564-7448*

The Christmas Shop
The Christmas spirit is alive and well in this festive shop that carries ornaments and decorations all year round. Many ornaments are made locally and in the USA while others are imported from Europe. *757-229-2514*

The College of William & Mary Bookstore and Café by Barnes and Noble
In addition to textbooks and school supplies, this bookstore carries Williamsburg clothing, books, souvenirs, William & Mary merchandise, greeting cards, stationery, newspapers, and periodicals. The café serves coffee, tea, sandwiches, pastries, and juices with tables located inside and out. *757-253-4900*

Danforth Pewter

Merging a colonial craft with contemporary design, this locally owned shop carries jewelry, oil lamps, housewares, ornaments, and more. *757-229-3668*

Everything WILLIAMSBURG

From T-shirts to toys, you'll find a broad selection of exclusive Colonial Williamsburg–logo products and souvenirs. Also shop for food and drinks, including exclusive Colonial Williamsburg beers, punch, and sodas. *757-565-8476*

French Twist Boutique

This boutique is French *and* local. The clothing is purely French. But, the French Twist showcases handmade accessories and jewelry that not only complement the designs but also give emerging designers a place to shine. *757-903-2755*

Hair of the DoG Bottle Shop

An extension of Chef David Everett's DoG Street Pub, this shop offers a wide selection of Virginia, imported, and domestic craft beers as well as cocktail mixers and gourmet foods. *757-903-4860*

J. Fenton Gallery

This gallery carries jewelry in sterling, glass, bronze, and mixed media; women's clothing, handbags, and hats; Radko glass ornaments; and Steinbach nutcrackers. *757-221-8200*

MERCHANTS SQUARE

Little is known about how the area now known as Merchants Square was used in the eighteenth century. There were probably residences and businesses catering to faculty and students of the nearby college. During the restoration of Williamsburg, many of the twentieth-century stores displaced from the eastern and central parts of town moved here, and it remains a commercial and shopping district. Merchants Square is listed by the National Register of Historic Places as an important example of an early planned shopping district.

Modvintique Interiors

Modvintique offers interior design consultation, home staging services, interior decorating, custom and ready-made window treatments, designer wallpaper and fabrics, antiques and collectibles, lamps, artwork, area rugs, specialty gifts, and home fragrances. *804-919-1488*

Ocean Palm

This specialty shop carries Palm Beach–style clothing, including Lilly Pulitzer apparel and accessories, Vineyard Vines, Barbour, and Sail to Sable. *757-229-3961*

The Peanut Shop of Williamsburg

Hand-cooked Virginia peanuts, specialty nuts, confections, old-fashioned bulk candy jars, regional specialty foods, and giftware are available in this local favorite. *757-229-3908*

The Precious Gem

This is a jewelry store like no other with custom jewelry by designer Reggie Akdogan, featuring diamonds and colored stones, including emeralds, rubies, and sapphires. *757-220-1115*

R. Bryant Ltd.

A Merchants Square fixture, this classic men's store has been serving discerning gentlemen looking for quality traditional menswear, imported and domestic, for nearly four decades. *757-253-0055*

R. P. Wallace & Sons General Store

Williamsburg T-shirts, souvenirs, jewelry, toys and gifts, nostalgic tin signs, bulk candy, and medicines are all for sale in this old-fashioned general store. *757-229-2082*

Scotland House Ltd.

Gifts and apparel from Scotland, Ireland, and England from cashmere sweaters to fine English pottery are available in this shop. *757-229-7800*

The Shoe Attic

With styles ranging from wild to elegant, this shop focuses on distinctive lines of high-quality women's shoes and accessories not found elsewhere in Williamsburg. *757-220-0757*

Shoesters
Shoes sold here are designed to fit the shape of the foot.
757-229-6999

Talbots
Talbots is a favorite with women everywhere, offering versatile sepa-
rates, sportswear, dresses, and fashion accessories. *757-253-6532*

Williams-Sonoma
The leading destination for home cooks in America offers cookware,
utensils, linens, cookbooks, dishes, glassware, specialty foods, and
ingredients. *757-220-0450*

WILLIAMSBURG At Home
Offering classic style for the modern home, WILLIAMSBURG At Home
carries an assortment of furnishings inspired by the artful archives of
Colonial Williamsburg. The sophisticated furnishings, including floor
coverings, bedding, and furniture, will complement any decor.
757-220-7749

WILLIAMSBURG Craft House
The iconic Craft House celebrates "yesterday inspiring today" with a
wide variety of folk art, gifts, personal accessories, and jewelry made
by modern artisans and tradesmen. Updated classics include exclusive dinnerware and tabletop patterns perfect for any wedding regis-
try. Machine engraving is available. *757-220-7747*

Wythe Candy & Gourmet Shop
A favorite of locals and visitors alike, the shop carries freshly dipped
caramel apples and chocolates, handmade fudge, and the region's
largest selection of candy. *757-229-4406*

Colonial Williamsburg is dedicated to the preservation, restoration, and presentation of eighteenth-century Williamsburg and the study, interpretation, and teaching of America's founding principles. The Foundation operates the 301-acre Historic Area and is the world's largest living history museum.

History

From 1699 to 1780, Williamsburg was the political, cultural, and educational center of the largest, most populous, and most influential of the American colonies. It was here that the fundamental concepts of our republic—responsible leadership, a sense of public service, self-government, and individual liberty—were nurtured under the leadership of patriots such as George Washington, Thomas Jefferson, George Mason, and Peyton Randolph.

Near the end of the Revolutionary War, the seat of government of Virginia was moved to the safer and more centrally located city of Richmond. For nearly a century and a half afterward, Williamsburg was a quiet college town, home of the College of William & Mary.

In 1926, the Reverend Dr. W. A. R. Goodwin, rector of Bruton Parish Church, shared with John D. Rockefeller Jr. his dream of

Reconstructing the wall
around the Capitol, 1933

preserving the city's historic buildings. Rockefeller and Goodwin began a modest project to preserve a few of the more important buildings. Eventually, their work expanded to include most of the colonial town, including the restoration of more than eighty of the original structures, the reconstruction of many buildings, and also the construction of extensive facilities to accommodate the visiting public.

Education Outreach

The Colonial Williamsburg Foundation actively supports history education through a wide variety of programs that engage students, teachers, and lifelong learners throughout the world.

Teacher Institute

Weeklong sessions and three-day themed seminars immerse teachers in an interdisciplinary approach to teaching social studies with American history and its relevance to today as the focus. These programs expand teachers' knowledge of our nation's founding principles, use a broad range of materials from primary sources to multimedia, explore American history from multiple perspectives, and provide innovative, experiential, and engaging strategies for bringing history to life in the classroom. Colonial Williamsburg offers programs both in Williamsburg and in teachers' home districts.

Education Resource Library

Colonial Williamsburg's education resource library features social studies and cross-curricular content for teachers and students, including dramatic video segments, student activities and games, classroom lesson plans, text and visual primary sources, and teacher guides. The material can be used to teach American history from Jamestown to the Civil War, social studies, and civics with cross-curricular ties to language arts, science, math, art, and music.

colonialwilliamsburg.org

Colonial Williamsburg's website provides a wealth of information about American history, the American Revolution, and life in colonial and Revolutionary Virginia. The site offers resources for teachers, students, and researchers and information on Colonial Williamsburg's collections.

**Teacher Institute participants
at the Carpenter's Yard**

School and Group Tours

The Historic Area offers various ways for groups of all sizes, interests, and ages to learn about American history. For more information on tours for school, including homeschool, groups as well as other youth and adult groups, call 1-800-228-8878 or email groupsales@cwf.org.

John D. Rockefeller Jr. Library

Through its specialized collections of books, manuscripts, archives, architectural drawings, images, and databases, together with its fellowship program and partnership with William & Mary Libraries, the Rockefeller Library supports and encourages research in the political and economic life of the thirteen colonies and the new Republic, the American Revolution, African American studies, historic trades, the decorative arts and material culture, archaeology, architectural history, the history of the restoration of Williamsburg, and historical preservation. Find more information on Colonial Williamsburg's education outreach programs at colonialwilliamsburg.org.

Colonial Williamsburg Publications

Trend & Tradition: The Magazine of Colonial Williamsburg

Colonial Williamsburg's illustrated quarterly tells the stories of eighteenth-century America from a twenty-first-century point of view. In addition to history articles about the colonial and Revolutionary eras, regular features highlight Colonial Williamsburg's art collections, offer cooking and crafts ideas, review new books, describe current and upcoming programs, and explore connections between our nation's beginnings and present-day events. The magazine is mailed to individuals and organizations that donate fifty dollars or more a year to the charitable, tax-exempt Colonial Williamsburg Fund. A sample of stories from each issue can be found at trendandtradition.org.

Books

Colonial Williamsburg publishes a wide variety of popular and scholarly books having to do with eighteenth-century history and culture. Categories of books include history, arts, archaeology, gardening, cooking, entertaining, crafts, decorating, and children's books.

Make a Difference: Giving to Colonial Williamsburg

Founded in 1926, The Colonial Williamsburg Foundation is a nonprofit educational institution and the largest living history museum in the United States. The Foundation receives no federal or state funding and instead relies on generous philanthropic initiatives in support of its mission: *to feed the human spirit by sharing America's enduring story.*

These charitable donations allow the Foundation to preserve more than six hundred restored and reconstructed buildings, curate and conserve our remarkable collection of early American art and material culture, provide world-class educational outreach programming, and present history so that visitors appreciate the lasting relevance of America's founding democratic principles in today's society.

By appealing to guests of all ages and demographics through a range of experiences, Colonial Williamsburg illuminates our nation's story so that we—as participants in this ongoing experiment in self-governance and enlightened citizenship—continue to learn from the people, events, and ideals that shaped America. More information on giving to the Foundation can be found online by visiting colonialwilliamsburg.org or by calling 1-888-293-1776.

INDEX

KEY

Restroom

Bus stop

Water

Cold drinks

Tickets

CAPITOL

R. CHARLTON'S
COFFEEHOUSE

RALE
TAV

NORTH